# FACING DEATH

ALSO BY ROBERT E. KAVANAUGH
*The Grim Generation*

# FACING DEATH

by
## Robert E. Kavanaugh

NASH PUBLISHING, LOS ANGELES

Library of Congress Catalog Card Number: 72-81842
Standard Book Number: 8402-1272-0

Published simultaneously in the United States and Canada
by Nash Publishing Corporation, 9255 Sunset Boulevard,
Los Angeles, California 90069.

Printed in the United States of America.

First Printing.

*My father passed away two months from the day I finished writing this book. As was his way, he gave mother a final order to turn off the television, and, as she moved to obey, he fell quietly asleep.*

*I loved him. We had no unfinished business. His time was right. Dad lived for his family. He had paid for seven sons through 167 years of schooling, largely in private institutions, but I never once heard him complain. Generosity was his name; it was a noble heritage for his family.*

*I would like to dedicate this book to Dad . . . and to his partner through fifty-one tough but happy years, my mother.*

*One week to the day after Dad's death, my sister-in-law Linda Bryson, died at thirty-seven in a small plane crash off Victoria Island, B.C. Her pilot husband tried valiantly to rescue her in near freezing waters, but went home alone to edit their newspaper and rear their seven children. I would like to include Linda in my dedication, and Jamie, her husband, and their wonderful children: Betsy, Bridget, Mark, Linda, Dinah, Heather, and baby Stuart, only nine weeks old.*

*Through these two personal experiences, I learned the value in facing death before its time, at first hand. My ideas are more than theories; they were tested in reality and they worked.*

# In Gratitude...

*To Patti, ex-widow, for being my wife and best friend.*
*To Su, who lost her dad and let me substitute.*
*To Jamie and Phil for being what brothers should be.*
*To Mary and Hugh for support and treasured friendship.*
*To my doctor, John Trombold, for our fun in learning together.*
*To Elisabeth Kubler-Ross whose research took the*
*   pennies off the eyes of the living so they could*
*   see the dying. . . .*

# Contents

# FACING DEATH

# 1.
# The American Scene: Dying and Death

When my time comes, I want to die with some degree of dignity, in peace and with purpose. I want the same death-style for my friends. Is this unrealistic? Must all of us look forward to that final entanglement of fear, deception and avoidance that surrounds so many Americans near death?

Strangely, interest in the subject of death is on the rise. Major magazines feature it. A national monthly recently reported half again as many respondents to a poll on death as to a poll on sex. Thirty-five students were forecast for my recent course on thanatology (the study of dying and death). More than 200 attended the first lecture.

Early in my professional studies of dying and death, my nights were regularly haunted by death-infested dreams. One night I dreamed I was close to the brink. Nobody had the courage to tell me. I simply knew.

Everyone special to me joined strange doctors and nurses

around the hospital bed. Bottles gleamed overhead. Tubes stretched everywhere. Two machines whirred nearby, gauges gauging, lights flashing red and white, bells tinkling softly.

Each person at bedside took a turn at cheering my future. One bearded doctor told gleefully of a new medicine with promise for my condition. A classic version of a head nurse, fluffing my pillow, described a breakfast I might never eat. My wife kept chattering about a European vacation, the shops and sights, the rest and restaurants. One brother talked of a book we could write together and another described an ocean cottage we might buy.

A Catholic priest kept popping in and out of the front row (I think I saw my mother pushing him from behind), asking timidly to lead a prayer service designed solely to restore health. Several times he reached to soothe my brow and once I felt traces of oil when he pulled his hand away. Then he left.

Not a smile lighted any face in the room. Intensity and glumness. Nobody would mention my plight or even hint at my condition. Nobody would take my hand. Nobody would squeeze my shoulder or return an honest gaze to help me face a shortened future. Even the vocabulary was septic. Words like "dying," "death," "terminal," " cancer," "autopsy" and "last rites" were not even whispered in my presence.

Friends not seen for years bobbed in and out of my view, now hiding their pale faces, now calling out pledges of love, of prayers, of undying friendship, of help with cash or anything. Anything at all that would not spoil the safety of their distance.

I am ashamed to go on, because I began to giggle in my dream. I had giggled before when dream-reality became too heavy to bear, when I was pushed beyond tears, beyond any usual expression of fear or grief. Mostly I can remember giggling the night I dreamed an atomic bomb had struck San Diego.

Now in retrospect, I understand my giggling as sanity's best reaction to this final rejection of my dignity as a man. Giggles climaxed in near hysteria as faces nearby wreathed in ever deepening seriousness and words of cheeriness and hollow holiness polluted the air. Then I noticed an undertaker friend smiling from the doorway.

My dreaming mind grew frenzied. Images raced by, caskets and graves, pallbearers and hearses, mourners and candles, tombstones and tears, vaults and black clothes. Flowers everywhere.

In a shattering and awakening insight, the truth dawned. To leave this life with any dignity and personal peace meant withdrawing from everyone and walking toward death alone. Near the edge, I was my sole human resource. My body would receive dedicated and expensive care. My feelings were my own.

A sense of isolation came, then soft tears. Not one friend would bestow his permission for me to die. Nobody near seemed brave enough to accept my final farewell or to impart his own. I hugged my sleeping wife while wondering how true this dream might be. A prophecy?

Deathbed scenes like this, where human dignity is affronted, are commonplace today. Actual scenes are not so compact as dreams, though they can be equally as impersonal, as ugly and cruel, as filled with fakery, evasion, cowardice and terror.

The majority of Americans can expect to die in a hospital or in a home for the aged. There, no brownie points are earned by doctors or by nurses for dealing humanely with the nonmedical aspects of dying. There is no special place on hospital charts or in nursing schedules for unplanned hours with dying patients and their families. The clear if unwritten goal in the institutions where most of us will die is: improve the patient's health, or if he is terminal, keep him quiet and comfortable until the end. And drugs are still the only way most health personnel know to keep the dying quiet and comfortable.

Close friends and even family members are tempted to stay away from the dying. They pretend their absence is to avoid being a nuisance when they are actually as relieved as most doctors and nurses to have any reasonable excuse for not confronting someone close to death. Highly moral people, who would almost prefer to die themselves than to lie and cheat, suddenly lose their ethical sense. Flowers, cards or gifts are as close as many dare come to a dying friend.

Recently, I heard a famous scientist boast that modern medicine has added more reality to the age-old concept of immortality than all the theologians and churchmen in history combined. In less than a century, medicine has added 25 years to man's span of life. Physicians seem determined to do almost anything to add still more years, willing at times to keep even one human system in working order when all others are defunct. Their skill and dedication are admirable, but man is so much more than one or several systems.

No matter how we measure his worth, a dying human being deserves more than efficient care from strangers, more than machines and septic hands, more than a mouth full of pills, arms full of tubes and a rump full of needles. His simple dignity as man should merit more than furtive eyes, reluctant hugs, medical jargon, ritual sacraments or tired Bible quotes, more than all the phony promises for a tomorrow that will never come. Man has become lost in the jungle of ritual surrounding death.

The consistently casual treatment of family members in

almost all hospitals proves that medicine does not yet consider the family an important factor in patient care. Families and friends of dying patients can become as bewildered and neglected as the patients themselves. Because of their lack of time, taste or training, doctors can be expected to encourage or counsel families only so far or so long. Doctors yield to busy nurses or maybe to chaplains, who in turn yield finally to morticians. And after a few days of expensive grief therapy, the morticians yield the family to the lonely agony of sidewalk therapy, the clumsy renewal of life without a loved one.

Americans have lost or abandoned any clear and universal customs that would afford the bereaved security and support around dying, death and funerals. We have lost hold on any guidelines for therapeutic mourning. Gone are the national and religious rituals for grieving, the wakes, the anniversary masses, the regular prayers, the proper clothing, post-funeral feasts. Cemeteries no longer have much magnetism and holidays for honoring the dead have less meaning and popularity each passing year.

Extended families, with aunts and uncles and cousins galore, are only rarely near or dear enough to offer more than token support before and after a relative expires. Neighbors generally seem less intimate and friendly, no more involved than box cakes, tuna casseroles or cut flowers. There are still warm and friendly congregations, but on the whole, churches are larger, less personal and increasingly less important to many. Rare is the church group that reflects a true sense of mission toward dying and mourning, while clergymen seem more willing each year to share their responsibilities with funeral directors.

Writing or teaching about thanatology, the study of human dying and death, is not easy. So many continue to see death as too morbid a topic, while others feign interest when they are only morbidly curious or guilty for the way they handled a suicide in their family. They block your words as they do the entire subject. Pages in books are passed over and classes are skipped with flimsy excuses. Professionals, like doctors, nurses, clergy and funeral directors, tend to don masks, pretending their experience has made them more skilled near death than factual studies reveal. Any candid approach to thanatology will necessarily blaspheme many of our primary cultural gods.

Our universal deity, Physical Health, is the major god currently offended. His demands for untold dollars in tribute are incessant. Every day it costs more to worship at his shrine, yet the devout seem only too willing to scrape and to pay. They sit uncomplainingly for endless hours in the offices of his high priests, and will purchase any drug or pill or lotion the priests prescribe, in any combination. In his shrine, the dying are excommunicated, the dead are damned.

The god of Youthful Appearance extracts perpetual care offerings from all of us perturbed by flabbiness, wrinkles and the growing creakiness in our bodies. Looking old or dead is a mortal sin. (Recently I have noticed that even youngsters look old when they are dying.)

The god of Sexual Attractiveness demands more than most dying folks can pay. Perfumes, cosmetics and hair-styling never seem quite enough, even when used with silk pajamas or sexy nighties. Fortunately, we have those prayer books for dreaming like *Any Woman Can*. On a recent visit to a home for golden years, I found an 84-year-old woman deeply engrossed in Dr. Reuben's book.

Our cultural god of Success is crucified at any deathbed scene with little promise of resurrection. Doctors seem to act out the futility of their best efforts and nurses seem sometimes reluctant to view an impending loss. Families continually experience the frustration of their inability to do more.

One god with a chance near death is Peace of Mind. His cause is often lost in a flurry of worship of the other gods. Yet, Peace of Mind can prevail. First, we need to find new values and styles of beauty in dying persons. Now we see only ugliness. For retrained eyes that see life more in perspective, there can be special and even radiant beauty in any human being who has himself all together on his death bed, peaceful, resigned and self-possessed.

I have observed this beauty in old and young alike, in religious people . and in ˙nonbelivers. They are at ease with themselves and with their world, seemingly ready for continued pain or imminent death. Loved ones have granted them permission to leave without any strings of guilt or dependency. Gradually, they have let go of every prize and person in the treasury of their concerns. Fear is minimal. Somewhere they have found the courage to face any future: reincarnation, a personal God or an endless sleep.

The period of time we now define as "dying" may well be one of the rare intervals in life when man can have the freedom to bring all his real values together, to be wholly himself and totally human. The relentless pressures from his culture and his life-style are nearly stilled. He can lower all barriers and face himself squarely. He can pare away the evasions in his life, the postponements, the excuses and denials, knowing at last who he is and whom he truly loves. For a while at least, he can become an integrated human person.

When expiration is clearly our sentence, all possessions and future planning lose their former luster. There are few tomorrows for feeding our worries. No reputation to earn or to bolster, no goals to achieve, no quotas to fill, no further use for power. There are no models to imitate, no enemies worth whipping, nobody to impress. Even envy for the living makes decreasingly less sense and greed has lost its purpose.

This image of harmony and peace in dying is more than an idealistic dream. Men best learn to die well by learning to live well. It is difficult but not impossible to learn even on our death bed. The key that unlocks serenity in the dying seems to be that poverty of spirit almost all religious or spiritual leaders recommend for life. It is an attitude of detachment from all that is not truly our own, learning to love persons without clinging or leaning unduly, and learning to possess material goods without greedy dependence. So much of the ugliness we fear near death is not physical at all. It is the spiritual ugliness of greediness to the end.

Helpful in dying a peaceful death, and maybe even essential at times, is the continued presence of a special someone who dares to walk to the edge with us. At the approach of death, the border between the world inside the head and the outside world grows blurred. A concerned confidant can help the patient remain in touch with reality. Mostly, a confidant will listen, allowing the patient to vent fears and second-guesses, lending support and encouragement while respecting privacy, sometimes confronting self-pity, always intent on helping the patient let go of all but what is truly his own.

When death becomes certain to follow, periods of depression are natural. They seem to be the patient's period for grieving the loss of himself. He mourns much as he will be mourned. Gradually, with the care of a confidant, patients can go beyond all paralyzing depression to a near constant state of resignation and acceptance. Resignation seems to flow naturally from the patient's increasing realization that his mind, his body, his memory, his loves, his satisfactions and talents still belong to him. And if man has an immortal soul, that, too, is his.

What more could there be? What more has there ever really been for the richest or the poorest? Total acceptance of all that truly belongs to us and the resultant resignation are obvious ways to face a basic truth in human experience: "You can't take it with you!" Whatever the "it" may be. For centuries, the pyramids and mausoleums of many cultures, filled with treasures, even with widows and servants, have stood as mute witnesses to this truth.

For many, a time in life arrives when death is more than inevitable. Death is right. A day dawns when life's tasks are largely finished and all living is downhill. Human powers have dwindled, loves are fully loved, duties all performed, fun and talent spent. Then most laughter echoes from the past, close friends are gone and tears dried up. On such a day, a man can rightly die. We know the wisdom in such thinking, since we say it often about all men but ourselves. How commonly we hear it whispered: "She is better off dead!" And we nod in concurrence.

When children die, however, no explanation human or divine quite hits the mark. Even promises of heavenly happiness are lost in man's ceaseless need to wonder "Why?" Fifty years ago our society was more in tune with children's deaths. Parents expected to lose one or more. Now the tragedy of youthful death causes unique anguish, capable of crippling survivors for many years. However, the youth of the deceased is defined in the eye of the bereaved, not in mine. Who is young? An octogenarian in good health may seem too spritely to die in the eyes of his widow. Who is young? No matter the calendar years, the young seem to be those who had an unfinished chapter in the plans of survivors.

Public opinion polls show Americans to be quite unanimous in their preference of sudden death. They want death to strike before they can fully realize what happened. We have no expert witnesses to testify from experience, but careful observers believe sudden death to be as painless as sudden and dreamless sleep. There appears to be little pain, little time for fear or for conscious feelings of any kind. Near victims of sudden death, the best witnesses we can find, tell of a built-in shock reaction that insulates against most pain. They tell, too, of almost total loss of recall during the tragedy.

Those who inordinately fear sudden death seem convinced of the pain and horror of it. They have only known the aftermath when death's wings brush by, the writhing in apparent pain, the blood and broken bones, the groans and grimaces. They hear the whisping inhalator or the patient gasping for breath. They see flashing red lights and hear the siren to and from. Most pain in sudden death is probably our own. Fears can stem from confusing the pain in our imagination with the actual pain experienced.

Sudden death may be more desirable for the victim, but it can cause painfully distinct problems for survivors. The shock and unreality are obvious, but besides, most comfort is offered when the surviving are too disorganized or disconsolate to profit. Later, when friends are needed for support in making a new beginning, they are tired of consoling, often misunderstanding the needs of the bereaved.

It is important to know that the process of human mourning begins when death is inevitable. During a lengthy terminal illness, the process of mourning begins when death is known to be the final outcome, or even when it is suspected. We can be thoughtlessly unkind to bereaved friends by failing to understand this difference. So often after a lingering illness, survivors feel only relief and we expect tears. They have already mourned for months or even years. They want no more from consolers than permission to begin a new life at once. No tears are left.

Television entered the American home only shortly after death was removed from the home to hospitals and funeral parlors. Television promised to be an ideal medium for death education, replacing grandfathers who used to die at home or family wakes where grandma rested in the living room. Television tried, oh, how it has tried! Over a two-week period of nighttime viewing, I counted an average of 34 deaths at close range, countless more at a distance. Not one death raised as much as a slight tremor in me. Television feeds our fantasy of forever being a spectator. Even a bloody nose or a fainting spell by a fellow viewer would have aroused more emotion in me than a hundred deaths on the tube.

The gradual decline of firm belief in orthodox religious creeds introduces a new dimension to dying for believers. In yesteryear, there was a higher percentage of believers and they appeared more childlike in their faith. Their uncluttered concern was heaven or hell, with purgatory for Catholics.

Now unshakeable faith is threatened by increasing uncertainties. Doubters and former believers are seemingly as happy as most believers. Change in religious practices long viewed as changeless bothers many. Astrologers and secular prophets tingle many a religious ear. Scientists again appear to be less traditionally religious. Now, rare is the sensitive believer who does not admit privately to suspicions that there are other possibilities after death.

Studies of the attitudes of religious people when dying reveal conflicting conclusions. It is a fact that numerous believers find serenity in their faith. Others find double trouble in their dying struggle. Besides the universal human fears, they seem too apprehensive about being well placed in afterlife. Fear of future punishment becomes a pre-occupation.

My conclusion is that religious faith of itself does little to affect man's peace near death. Worry warts are worry warts no matter their theology. It is not the substance or content of a man's creed that brings peace. It is ·the firmness and quality of his act of believing. Firm believers, true believers, will find more peace on their deathbeds than all others, whatever the religious or secular label we place on their creed. The believer, not the belief, brings peace.

Whether his faith is in the supremacy of a personal God or in the dignity of a godless man, the true believer experiences a tranquillity while dying not seen in nonbelievers, or in those who believe fearfully because of family tradition or childhood memories. Part of the reason we cannot see clearly the validity of secular believers is because the majority of tales about dying men come from religious sources. Churches had a vested interest in publicizing the dying peace of saints and martyrs. They did not tell how dissolute kings or heretics also died peacefully, yet many did, and their counterparts in our times still do, if they are true believers. True believers are men committed to any set of transcendant values and who dare live them to the end.

Interest and curiosity about the subject of death are every-where. Since my course on thanatology was announced, my mail is dotted with clippings, poems, unfinished manuscripts by the dead, suicide notes, invitations to be cremated or to join a memorial society, ghoulish letters, and tons of re-ligious literature.

Of special interest is the curiosity of the young about death. They talk glibly of it, romanticize it in song, pontifi-cate on the irreverence and waste in funeral customs, absorb it on the screen. All the while they studiously avoid or are judiciously spared much actual contact with real death. An extensive poll I conducted among college students revealed that 78 percent had yet to see a dead person up close. More than 92 percent had yet to witness a death.

Working on a college campus, I used to pooh-pooh my generation gap, until a class project required my hiking through an old cemetery with several youngsters. I scrupulously stepped around each grave, respecting its sacredness as taught, inwardly fearful of sinking. My companions trooped merrily everywhere, not a single hangup in evidence. Have our young lost all sense of reverence for the sanctity of cemeteries, frolicking, laughing, whooping, where silence or quiet are warranted? Or is there a new sense of the sacred in the air? My generation respected burial grounds by day and necked there by night. For my young associates cemeteries could easily be playgrounds or parks by day and concert grounds by night. They neck in public.

In the majority of death-related attitudes, the young are not too unlike their elders. For both, the mushroom cloud of an atomic bomb always rests on a distant horizon. Never overhead. The magic rug of omnipotence hovers handily nearby, ready for instant escapes into fantasy whenever death becomes too close or too real. Forever spectators, never participants! At least until tomorrow.

At the recent funeral of an alcoholic friend, the eulogizer told more lies than are told at a devil's convention. Virtues my friend could neither spell nor pronounce were attached to his past life by one of that new breed of clergymen, hearse chasers, who make it big by rescuing churchless families from the shame of a nonreligious funeral.

As we left the chapel, resentment and shame pervaded the crowd. Everyone needed to laugh out his embarrassment, but nobody could. Relatives slunk furtively away. Personally, I resented the clergyman's rudeness in forcing his narrow beliefs on the friends of a confirmed unbeliever. Friends were teased into tears when in fact they were relieved by the death of a man who had suffered too long.

What purpose could such a funeral serve? Are clergymen needed at such funerals when they have nothing special to offer? Present in the congregation were two dozen professional men and women who could have eulogized more fittingly, if clumsily. Why a funeral at all? Do any funerals serve a purpose except maybe in small towns? Or are they remnants of a day when families were closer, when neighbors were friends or friendly enemies instead of strangers?

Writing this book has not been easy. Friends hear you are writing, inquire avidly about the subject, then gulp and look away when you tell them. No wonder death is now known as the new pornography and Americans as the new Victorians of prudery about death. Some days I feel like the teller of bawdy jokes in a girl scout camp or convent parlor.

I wrote this book for two reasons. First, in an effort to help those to gain new peace who, like myself, feel fearful and uneasy around dying and death. Hopefully, by sharing the thoughts of one who sinks when he tries to walk on water, they might find motivation to face mortality with new honesty and courage. Perhaps, too, they might learn how to mourn therapeutically and to aid the grief-stricken in ways that are truly effective.

My second reason for writing was to encourage those fearful of dying to live their daily lives with more zest and fulfillment. Zest can result from realizing that death-centered fears are often no more than fears of living in disguise. For example, people who admit to an undue fear of the unknown in death undoubtedly live in daily fear of the unknown in all novelty and change. Unwilling to take any risks or to venture along untrod paths in life, they compel friends around them to undertake all risks and to lead in all changes. They lack adventure and excitement. Their fear comes out in boredom and fantasy.

Reflection on death has taught me that fulfillment in life can only come from defining clearly what we want before death. What is the "it" we ceaselessly seek? Is it wealth? Is it fame? Is it seeing our children well placed in life? Is it a contribution to science or writing a book? Look at the dying of any age whose only tomorrow is loneliness and pain. Hear how they plead for one more day, convinced they will discover "it." Growing awareness of what we hope to achieve in life can bring fulfillment to daily living, some perspective to our choices and will allow for peaceful resignation when death beckons. The most miserable men near death are those who had no clear aims in life or whose aims were beyond any human achievement.

These pages do not pretend to unravel the mystery of death. Alexis Carrel speaks of mysteries that are knowable or unknowable. Death is of the latter kind. At least nothing I have read or discovered has hinted differently. My excuse for adding my own reflections to an already massive literature is the hope that you might find courage here to face the mystery of death, and your reward, like mine, will be the art of more graciousness around death.

No anger prompts me to launch into diatribes against professional villains who keep dying and death from being less than human. For years I resented funeral directors, those popular whipping boys, especially the kind who park their private hearses nearby while they perform the public and elected office of coroner, profiteering on their office and on the confusion of the newly bereaved. Now even that anger has subsided.

I find that, in reality, funeral directors differ greatly from their public image. Unlike other service people who allegedly overcharge for services—such as physicians, plumbers, mechanics and electricians—funeral directors are always instantly available, and usually kind. Their influential role in death affairs is less a matter of their untoward motives than of our national unwillingness to deal openly with death. Funeral directors began in America as a combination of three professions needed at time of death: cabinetmakers, livery stable men and sextons. Now they are nudging out other professions, often by default, becoming cosmeticians, psychological therapists, part lawyer and insurance advisor, part clergyman and businessmen.

I feel no anger toward physicians. Their role with dying persons and families grows daily more complex. Questions about transplants, euthanasia and drug usage complicate the traditional tasks of telling the patient his plight and counseling the family. Many physicians are specialists who first meet the dying patient and saddened family only shortly before or after the fatal quality of the illness is known. Few doctors now in practice had any special training in the human or emotional aspects of dying and grieving. Yet, many specialists have dozens of dying patients in their clientele. One hematologist friend of mine tells of burying 18 patients in a single month.

Nor do I harbor anger for hospital staffs or for men of the cloth. Their sometime failure to face the human needs of the dying or grief-stricken is representative of our culture. They are you and I in uniform. To point out their faults is to misunderstand that rarely were they trained or even encouraged to do what they know needs doing near death.

My only impatience is with our combined and continuing evasion of the reality of human life and its needs near termination. My impatience abounds when I repeatedly confront our national refusal to treat man as man deserves until the end, with dignity and even some nobility. His is an abiding right to die well and to be buried respectfully, as he chooses. I long for the day when our impropriety at death will be transformed into a celebration of life.

I have no illusions that all will want to die in a similar way. At a national conference, I heard a young black woman say: "I have been a rebel all my life. Death is my enemy, the enemy of my people, it stalks our ghetto. I will fight and rebel against this enemy to the end. And if any of you present want to help me die in dignity, keep me from being resigned or peaceful. I am a fighter." I realize, too, that worriers obtain much satisfaction from their worries. After a lifetime of practice, they will hardly want to stop their fretting when dying. My hope is that each man can find the emotional freedom to face death as he chooses, with the particular serenity that is his own.

Early in life Mother informed me: "Whatever in life is worth doing, is worth doing well." I bought this maternal wisdom and I still do. Dying well is worth it, because it will insure I lived well, too. I am convinced that our personal failures to unearth, face, understand and accept our true feelings about death keep us from joyful living and dying as we choose. Our failures likewise keep us from treating those we love who are dying with the dignity they deserve.

# 2.
# Confronting
# Death-Related Feelings

Aside from stamping ants on sidewalks, my first experience with death, as best I can recall, happened in early second grade. Several of the seven Kavanaugh brothers found our dog, Sandy, dead and nearly frozen in the woods behind our house. Crow hunters had done it. By accident, we hoped.

Sandy was no ordinary dog. He had seven young masters for loving and teasing, for wrestling and obeying. Dad was his big boss and Sandy abandoned everyone else when Dad beeped the car horn to the tune of "Shave and a Haircut, Two Bits." Sandy feared Mother who broomed him into the basement each night, yet he loved her because she fed and watered him.

My shock and sadness came out in private tears. Anger came and jealousy, too. I almost hated the man who offered a puppy in quick replacement. I watched other dogs, wondering why Sandy had had to die instead of those mutts.

Rage came out in our late night plans to stalk the next hunting party we saw. However, the best grief therapy was in planning and performing a solemn high mass for Sandy's funeral.

After all, Sandy was a Catholic. While playing priest we had baptized him, laughing at his muskrat look as water oozed over his head, admiring his obedience when the lighted baptismal candle touched his paw and blessed salt touched his long tongue. Playing bishop, we had confirmed him, too, complete with olive oil and a sound slap on the cheek. Often we slipped him a white Necco wafer, the color nobody liked, when he looked hungry at communion time.

I wonder if any canine requiem could ever compare to Sandy's. Three youthful self-ordained priests presided, one eulogized. His cardboard casket was covered with a black pall, lowered away to an off-key Gregorian chant. Mother made the priestly vestments, and we served lots of his favorite Necco wafers, white ones, to all the Protestant kids who came to gawk. We buried him in ground blessed with our own homemade holy water. Then we rolled a huge rock over his grave.

In retrospect, it all sounds so cute and boyish. At the time it was not. It was sad and upsetting, somewhat frightening. I felt uneasy digging a grave, lifting my dead dog, throwing dirt over him, all the while wondering if there might be a dog heaven. My teacher, Sister Mary, said there well could be. I think I prayed for Sandy every time we walked along the path where we laid him, in case there was a purgatory for dogs, too.

Our past lives are invariably dotted with Sandy-like scenarios. Yet, most Americans have no more than shadowy indications of their true feelings about death. Ask friends how they feel about dying or death, and you will hear how they would like to feel or how they think they ought to feel. Our society frowns on any open discussion of so gruesome a topic. Actual feelings remain buried within secret caverns of the self, never fully searched out, so never squarely faced or fully experienced.

Psychologists increasingly insist that our death-related emotions affect the quality and the style of our daily life. They can influence the way we drive a car, our habits of eating and drinking, the way we exercise. How much we sleep, what pills or drugs we use, our spirit of adventure, even the degree of our commitment in love can all be severely affected by hidden and unresolved qualms about death. A good example is insomnia, where restful sleep is difficult because it is feared as an imitation of death. We become especially aware of our feelings as they seem to surface and ignite unaccustomed turbulence when we feel obligated to visit a friend who has terminal cancer, or attend a poignant funeral.

While I was teaching an extension course at the University of California at San Diego on thanatology, it became clear to me that an honest and humane approach to death can begin only when we allow ourselves to get in touch with our visceral *feelings*. Otherwise, any stance we adopt toward death will be no more than another form of blocking and avoiding honest confrontation. It is not the dying or the dead we fear as much as the unknown and untested *feelings* they evoke within ourselves.

A well-known biochemist liked to advertise his fearlessness during a recent bout with death. While describing this experience to my class, however, his usually bombastic manner faded into an unfamiliar softness. His loud and energetic voice constricted into a wistfulness barely audible beyond the first few rows. Never had I heard my friend so controlled.

In my classes, students regularly mocked adult fears and what they felt was our undue concern with the individual's inevitable end. I mistook their bravado for bravery until I realized how many of them were rapping on death as they did on sex, merely as interested virgins. Rarely had they lost someone close or yet known a relationship seasoned by years of mutual intimacy from which they might imagine the grief that such a human loss can bring. Inexperience and a sense of being special, even omnipotent, left them unable to get beyond head trips in our class discussions.

Older students who professed no fear of death were often strangely unable to attend regular class sessions where articulate men spilled unalloyed feelings about death and afterlife. Excuses were amusing. Even among those attending, an abundance of glassy eyes suggested their minds too frequently were on jaunts to more pleasant subjects.

Death does not permit objectivity. At birth it is too late. All of us are subjectively involved, because each of us is always dying. Those we designate as "dying" differ only in that they know the nearness, while all know the inevitability. We assume a variety of masks to pretend we are objective when we only mean we are controlled. The basic mask all humans put on is to call ourselves "the living," when we are equally "the dying."

Doctors and nurses can use white uniforms and speak their Greek-rooted gobbledygook instead of clear English. Stethoscopes, pain-killers, thermometers, bandage changing, tube arranging, busy schedules, endless charts and hierarchical buck-passing, all are important parts of a routine designed to help them remain a few steps away from raw confrontation with expiring patients.

Clergymen, too, have face-saving escapes. Clerical garb, titles and unfamiliar language can keep patients at a distance.

Ritual sacraments, Bible readings, silent prayers and hospital rules can rescue uneasy clergymen from any but casual involvement.

Funeral directors use a host of clever shields against each fresh contact with open grief. They have invented an entire language of euphemisms and they gently force the bereaved to learn and speak it. Canned advice and inspirational quotes may sound spontaneous to each new mourner when they are only planned techniques to avoid words from the heart. Mourners are kept busily engaged in deciding, selecting, signing papers, always in a routine neatly designed to prevent emotions from erupting.

Honest laymen know these facades. They mutter at the ghastliness of visiting open caskets or how, if dying, they would want to be left alone, thus enabling them, reasonably and righteously, to stay away from both the dead and the dying. Laymen know, too, of reverse masks, where grief is feigned for business purposes and funerals are used as fine occasions to meet the proper people.

Society recognizes that there are times when every human being needs to don a mask. Medics may unashamedly wear theirs when wards or caseloads reek too heavily of dying. Clergymen and morticians properly feel guiltless when demands surpass their personal strength. Human limitations require that we invest only so much of self in the loss and grief of others. No man can rightfully tell another how far to push himself.

Honest recognition of our latent feelings about human mortality enables us to be free enough to make some choices. Only when we know our feelings can we respect our unique reactions. No longer need we pummel and even smash our emotional selves behind artificial defenses. Once free, we can choose the masks we want or need, even sometimes going maskless, instead of compulsively avoiding the reality of all death and grief because we lack the humility and courage to be any other way.

Most people I observe don their masks compulsively. Some of our masks are cruel, demeaning, inflammatory or actually harmful to patients and families, reflecting a coldness we do not feel, a curtness, an indifference, a sense of being too busy. Once we become aware of our rigid, compulsive behavior, we may start to find some freedom of choice, and alternative stances are possible. Professionals and laymen can select a shield that fits the situation, respecting personal needs and limitations and the needs of folks they visit. It helps immensely for professionals to inspect the mask they wear, encouraging honest feedback from patients or families. Those who believe their traditional stance is one of objectivity may soon learn how narrow the line is between objectivity and coldness.

Even uniquely strong human beings rarely reach a consistently comfortable and gracious posture in the presence of human death. No matter how many patients they visit or tend, no matter how many times they are partners in grief, their unresolved feelings cause internal distress and withdrawal behind their pretenses of warmth and concern.

No books or conferences, no movies or discussions, will be effective, ultimately, in helping us master the art of peace and graciousness near death, until we permit our feelings to be honestly and fully felt, and admit it is all right to feel as we do. Until then, newly acquired skills will be no more than fresh evasions.

Only some uneasiness and fear will disappear when we succeed in opening up. Much will remain as part of our cultural heritage. We will not grow instantly brave, only gradually less fearful of being human, of owning up to the reality of self. What is so wrong with feeling a modicum of fear and uneasiness without running to hide? Such feelings are as normal and natural as death.

Once we discover the nature and extent of our visceral feelings, it helps to counterattack. It facilitates growth to experience what we fear without trying so hard to mask our reactions. Uneasy in the presence of the dying? Visit them and stay longer than needed. Fearful of open tears? Visit grief-stricken friends. Uncomfortable at wakes and funerals? Go! And soon we will find that others can accept our clumsiness whenever we can. In fact, the clumsiness of professionals and friends grants to patients and their families permission to exhibit tears and awkwardness they never dared display before.

I would prefer the clammy or trembling hand of someone than no hand at all. In fact, I would never know if the moisture and shakes were theirs or mine. I would prefer a doctor who stuttered and lost some dignity in tears than to be continually chilled by professional aloofness. I would rather a friend came and dumped his own fears than to grieve alone or with too fearless a friend. I could gain far more from a mortician with a real tear in his eye and a real quiver in his voice than from one with impeccable control and modulated emotions. Humaneness triggers humaneness. Warmth generates warmth. For practiced and unpracticed alike, it is normal to feel uneasy around death. And it is not abnormal to admit or show it.

I can recommend two approaches helpful to many in exposing death-related feelings. First, a reflective journey back through life, focusing carefully on experiences that possibly formed present attitudes. If your early life, prior to this time, has been touched by death, you may well capture again many of the original emotions. Clues will arise as to what is buried inside, what was never fully experienced before, what is unfinished grief, as distance lends courage and perspective not had before.

Those with few or no death-tinged experiences in their past, will undoubtedly find the vacuum now filled with fantasies grown up out of ignorance, suspicion, invention or hearsay. Maybe fantasies were ballooned out of proportion by horror movies, or murder mysteries. Their fears may be no more than echoes of other people's fears, easily dispelled by their own first-hand experiences.

A second approach I value consists in carefully reflecting on death fears admitted by others. Any list of such fears contains common chords, major and minor. By careful sorting and musing, by discussion and the refusal to run away, can come the freedom and permission to own what we truly fear. To buy into our deep-seated fears is to begin to deal therapeutically with them, to dissipate some, while insuring others will not force us into a phony or compulsive stance when death comes close.

The remainder of this chapter contains my own reflections on death in my past. Hopefully, my thoughts can serve as facilitators to your own. My attempts at honesty might unleash yours. In the following chapter, I report an interview with an exceptional woman who willingly shared the litany of fears she identified in living and in dying.

Shortly after the funeral of our dog Sandy, Sister Bridget, my third grade teacher, appointed me an altar boy. I recall serving at my first funeral early in third grade, the first of more than 400. Another altar boy and I accompanied our priest to the home where the casket lay in the living room, banked by flowers. As Father blessed the body and lowered the lid, I peeked in for my first glimpse of a human corpse. It was an old man I had never seen before. When the finality of the thudding lid caused a chorus of moans and sobbing tears, shivers went up and down me, all over.

Spookiness best describes my feelings, and thereafter, every association with death took on a spooky air. Funeral homes, coffins, dying people, hearses, cemeteries, old-age homes and floral shops alike! At that time I began to trade purple jelly beans, because they tasted to me the way funerals smelled.

Father led the funeral procession to church, flag on fender, motorcycle policeman directing; I felt terribly important. During mass I kept glancing back at the casket in the center aisle, also eyeing the mourners sobbing in the front pews. After mass I held Father's cope as he circled the casket, sprinkling holy water and incensing the body. The more I tried avoiding the casket, the more I bumped it. And spookiness each time.

It was a relief to sit down for the sermon by our Monsignor, but not for long. It was the shortest funeral sermon I have ever heard.

In fairness, you should know a mite about Monsignor before you hear of his sermon. Armed with an episcopal mandate to inspire our parish with the best in good example, Monsignor led us back from the scandal of a neighboring pastor marrying his housekeeper and the still greater scandal of our own pastor being killed by the gun of his crazed assistant pastor. Monsignor took his leading seriously, especially at funerals.

Picture this steely-haired cleric standing in the opening of the communion railing, staring in silence at the casket for fully a minute. Slowly pointing his finger at the casket, and in his mildest snarling tone, he fairly growled: "If the top of that casket suddenly popped open and old John sat up, he wouldn't know where he was. He was never inside this church a day in his life. Pray for him! In the name of the Father and of the Son and of the Holy Ghost. Amen." Amen! Things were different then. You can guess who was ahead of me in the line outside Monsignor's confessional the next Saturday. John's widow.

In primary grades, we learned a lot about hell, a little about heaven and loads about purgatory. Purgatory was as high as most dared aspire. Each night I concentrated fervently on my act of contrition, hoping it would prove perfect enough to avoid hell if I died during the night like so many kids did in the scary stories Sister told. The list of people I needed to pray for lengthened nightly, including every relative and friend, nuns and priests, garbage men and new bus drivers. To forget a name meant putting them in spiritual jeopardy and me in danger of purgatory for not loving properly.

Through grade and high school, I averaged three funerals per month. We went less and less to homes, increasingly to funeral homes, until undertakers replaced priests as casket-closers, then we only went to church. Such relief. Nothing so adversely affected my attitudes toward death as the wails and groans when caskets were closed and sometimes reopened, occasionally over and over, until every bystander was paralyzed in tears, including one little altar boy.

Usually I cried too at Italian funerals or when taps echoed for vets. Rarely did I know the deceased, but at less emotional funerals I felt guilty for not shedding a tear. I confessed my failing and my confessor assured me it was no sin. "It is normal not to cry for strangers."

At times we accompanied Father on early morning communion calls to the bedridden. We knelt next to the bed, reciting the Latin confiteor and holding the paten under the chins of nuns, the crippled, mental patients, the aged of every description, many about to die. The nuns looked funny with linen bonnets pulled over badly shaved heads, solving a mystery for one who always wondered what Sister did with her hair.

During altar boy days, I witnessed the grief-style, funeral customs and burial procedures of every type of family in our parish melting pot. We buried Slavs and Italians, Poles and Mexicans, Germans and Irish, French and Indians, Orientals and those of African ancestry. I learned how it was done for politicians and bishops, for nuns and priests, for babies and children, for vagrants and entire families, for veterans of World War II.

Highly influential in forming my feelings were the scenes at graveside. Italian mothers sometimes threw themselves on the casket and had to be pried loose. Relatives would beg for a final look at the deceased and collapse in hysteria. Tears were always louder, sobbing harder. More than once I was needed to tote a vagrant to his final resting place, no friends for pallbearers, no funds for stand-ins, no parishioners available. Even the most stoic families were driven to open grief by the sight of a gaping grave and piles of dirt.

No relief could equal mine when Father closed his Latin book and moved toward the final handshake with the next of kin. That was every altar boy's signal to break for Father's car, escaping the awful lowering of the casket and the tenseness of dirt on concrete.

Alice Dickens sat in front of me in fifth grade before she died. As the entire fifth grade marched in ranks to Donovan's Funeral Home for her rosary, I regretted teasing her, stuffing her pigtails in my inkwell and muttering under my breath when she tried to recite. As Hail Marys droned on, I craned to see her in the coffin. Afterwards, my friend Sammy nudged me to stay. When nobody was noticing, he touched her hand, daring me to do the same. But I was afraid. For many nights afterwards I tossed in bed, imagining her hand in mine. And her hand was cold and dead.

I can still remember seeing shiny black hearses, curtained, mysterious, gliding down our street, pausing in front of houses, finally stopping, body carried out, casket carried in, floral marker on the door, people trooping in and out, then draped windows and black clothes for many months. One of our tribe of seven brothers reluctantly took mother's meatloaf and chocolate cake to the door, peeking inside. (Once baby Danny asked if dead people ate meatloaf and chocolate cake.) For hours the neighborhood gang would congregate across the street, down aways, peering, looking nonchalant, hoping to glimpse a dead body, fearing we might.

When our grandmother lay dying—we called her "Ma"—six little boys stood and squirmed outside her door in the hallway of her flat, while an even smaller one crawled along the floor. Uncles and aunts were generous with nickels for being good which meant being quiet. Sometimes we opened Ma's door for a "Hi, Ma!" but Ma never returned our "Hi!" She looked awful. The doctor came with his black bag and showed us his colored pills. Father came for Latin prayers and we knelt respectfully. Then they took us to Aunt Vern's and everyone said Ma was dead.

Ma looked almost alive in her casket and it was not spooky at her funeral. Her grandsons served, and even when I bumped her casket nothing happened. After all, Ma was inside. I knew and loved her. Even the cemetery was not sinister when Pa and Mother and my aunts cried. I think I cried, too.

One night at supper, Dad announced I had just been offered a job with one of his friends. Night watchman and clerk at a funeral home. The only duties were answering the phone, a little dusting and watching for prowlers.

My new boss showed me his palatial mortuary. I closed my eyes in the casket display room, lowered them and held my breath in the embalming room and secretly held my nose as we inspected the chapels where flowers surrounded two caskets. He showed me the tiny office where I would await grief in the night. Outside the window, two black hearses stood poised for my command. The pay sounded good. Dad never understood why I never began, probably accusing me in his own mind of ingratitude instead of the real reason: the place spooked me.

One Sunday evening a bad accident happened on our corner. Dad carried one victim inside, laying him on the davenport under a blanket. He was bleeding badly when men came to take him away. Nobody told me but I believe he died on our couch. Whenever Mother was gone long enough for us to wrestle in the living room, I always tumbled my opponent off the davenport, quickly.

Outwardly it was fun the Halloween we dared to "Trick or Treat" at a funeral home. Laughing boisterously, we knocked until the undertaker came. He invited us to wait inside while he solemnly departed along a darkened corridor to a distant room. On a dare, I opened the door where he had been. The naked body of an old woman lay on the embalming table and even now I feel guilty for invading her privacy.

Cemeteries were eerie places for me and my friends. One summer I worked trimming around tombstones, memorizing "Casey at the Bat" and most of Robert Service and Edgar Allan Poe while snipping around old graves. I did not often join our gang in their necking parties inside the Protestant cemetery. I knew only Catholic cemeteries were consecrated ground, but I am not certain now whether sacredness, spookiness or girls were more frightening.

At age seventeen I entered the seminary which admiring friends slippingly called the cemetery. My new status kept me out of the draft for World War II. I felt guilty over those years when seven schoolmates were killed, and doubly so when their mothers hugged me at their wakes, telling me how lucky my mother was to have me far away from war and death.

Little did those grieving women know how truly far removed the seminary was from the global conflict and carnage. My life view narrowed into a narcissistic concern for: my studies, my sports, my health and my spiritual life. My solipsism-in-action earned me the family title of "King Seminarian." Once we sang at a bishop's funeral, once we waked and buried our rector, and once we buried an elderly nun whose path to sanctity was in the seminary kitchen. My distance from all dying grew and religion added new controls. In nostalgic backward glances, I now see the seeds of the avoidance methods so many clergymen use.

Our seminary specialized in avoidance. No contact with the outside world beyond the daily sports page on the bulletin board or a box of cookies from home. We were encouraged to sever every important human tie, any bonds that would make parting painful, in the interest of serving all men equally. In their zeal to mold us into men of that world where death has no victory, our spiritual directors concentrated their fire on our cliques and close friendships as well as family relations.

Later, we spent months studying the last rites and all the bizarre circumstances we might face. Accident victims along the highway, people entrapped in tunnels or fiery buildings, prisoners hanged or electrocuted, soldiers maimed in battle. We schemed endlessly of different ways to approach backsliders or to talk the reluctant into receiving the sacraments. Practicing for rites that could change men's eternities without once coming within miles of a dying person! All theory, no laboratory.

Our moral theology professor clocked our dash to the spiritual rescue, unable to pass unless we could complete the last rites in less than 45 seconds. Later I knew the value in such training. Catholics expected quickie sacraments and rarely complained. They usually believed the last rites might achieve what they never were intended to do: rectify the relationship of an unconscious or dead man with his God. Relatives applauded the briefest visit, always understanding "How busy you are, Father," even when we sneaked into a morgue to anoint a cold body under the theological theory that souls might not leave bodies for at least three hours after medical death.

Our seminary offered no lessons on facing the dying patient as a human being with fears and maybe terror. No skills were imparted on how to assist the bereaved. I brought little more understanding to my early sick calls than Mother had taught at home: Be kind, gentle and thoughtful, As I ran quickly in and out of homes and hospitals, to accidents or tragedies, reading Latin prayers, absolving, anointing, another set of conflicting values rose within me. I began to feel the need to stay and mourn a while, to chat and listen a bit, to say English prayers, to serve as a sounding board for the grief of frightened men and women, dying or grieving.

The human anguish around the dying could be "honorably" bypassed with hurried rites and flimsy excuses. Any excuse Father offered was a holy one. Soon I believed the dying were often more in need of present comfort than of forgiveness for the future. Slowly and painfully, my needs to stay near the deathbed won out. I remember the night of the final breakthrough.

In the polio epidemic of 1953, I stood all night with a family of nine while number ten, a seventeen-year-old girl, struggled in an iron lung. She watched in a mirror as the ten of us rose in unison, heel and toe, toe and heel, matching

35

each whisping breath of that giant machine. She refused the last rites, satisfied with the comfort human presence could bring. Then she died.

Despite an all-night vigil, I needed no extra sleep. A new buoyancy came from attacking my fears. Still feeling spooky inside, still cowardly and conditioned to run to a quiet rectory, I finally found the courage to stay and be afraid. Now it was possible to confront death head-on with only inward apprehension and no evasion. I could even cry in front of people. Now the only problem was when to leave a deathbed scene. No books told. There were few models to imitate and little counseling from peers who largely followed the "quickie" route.

Most of my priestly work was among college students. No death seemed more tragic than the suicide of a bright nineteen-year-old, unless it was the death of a beauty queen from a clumsy and illegal abortion. Nothing in the world of the young offered a single clue to understanding death. It was easy for a frightened man to be a hero in the land of the naive. My mission was less difficult because of a burning conviction that death meant mere entrance into eternal happiness, possible even for Protestants, Jews and non-believers. This conviction eased my fears. It did not remove them.

Death struck personally close when twice I heard my surgeon say: "I think we got it all." The "it" both times was beginning cancer. On neither occasion was death a remote prospect. Maybe unreality came from my being employed by God. Maybe from the joviality of the surgeon whose favorite mask was joking. Most likely, death seemed unreal because it never happened to spectators like me.

The final and most decisive experience occurred in my adult life. A very close friend and I were hospitalized at the same time. One afternoon he suggested a stroll around the park-like grounds, but hospital schedules prevented my joining him. That night I heard the news that this brilliant, athletic and strikingly handsome priest, thirty-six years of age, had been found dead in the woods. Hospital authorities announced that he had slipped and hit his head on a rock. I thought differently. His parents were arriving the following day and he feared telling them of his desire to leave the priesthood. Nobody in authority knew his faith had dwindled, maybe disappeared. I was the last human being to see him alive. Nobody asked me a question. The Catholic authorities at the hospital and in his religious order believed what they needed to believe: it was an accident.

Reflecting on this tragic waste of human beauty and goodness, I knew life *here* was paramount. Had my friend requested a sacrament from me, hospital rules would not have stopped me. He asked instead for a human presence, and I was not there. I did not then shed my belief in afterlife, rather I began to comprehend how much less it mattered.

Now outside the norms of traditional theology and church discipline, I find it frightening at times to live without instant explanations for death. It has been comforting in the past to explain tragic death in terms of divine justice, citing God's permissive will. For the first time I feel the perplexity and futility of all who listened to my former explanations. Now I realize they listened more to me and my concerns than to my endless words.

Pressure to accept easy explanations grows greater now as the body ages, losing its vitality, with creaking joints, saggings everywhere, constant bruises and perdurable aches. The signs of aging are only real when they happen to yourself. Recently I noticed how the mirror only reflects my face. Faces grow old gradually, almost imperceptible to the owner.

The softening of my official and clerical stance permits a more balanced view of the entire subject of human mortality. I better understand unbelievers and undertakers, forlorn husbands and fatherless children, doctors and suicide victims. No longer do I view every tragic death in a religious context before it is humanly felt. For the first time, I find hospital and burial bills real. Priests were healed and buried at discount.

To dying and bereaved friends, I offer no magic or myths, few consoling words. Myself is all I have to offer, my freedom, my fear and uneasiness, my warmth and concern, my willingness to hear any viewpoint, even despair. I have no oils for anointing, but my hand can be held. No ritual to read, but my eyes can return an honest gaze. No busy schedule, only time to sit near the bed of anyone I love, or maybe in a corner, offering presence in their privacy. No need to fear my uniform or even fear shocking me with outlandish beliefs or blasphemous attitudes.

Now I have a family and can allow people near me to need and want me. I can openly admit I do not want to go away. Gone is the posture of false bravado and omnipotence. At last I feel human enough to die.

A personal God may be one breath away. If so, I will try to love Him as I try to love the folks I meet each day. I cannot believe He cares about my rejecting or adopting a creed that will not alter my life. Nor that oils and blessings with a few muttered words can change my eternity. Any credible God will understand the search of one who believed before he switched to Pablum, who prayed before he said "da, da" clearly and who blessed himself before he walked.

So much for my experiences and reflections. Before reading further, I suggest you pause and spend whatever time you need to put your death-affected experiences in focus. Allow yourself to feel what you feel. It can be painful to see again your dying cat, your puppy hit by a car or to relive your grandpa's funeral. It hurts to recall an accident that killed your favorite friend or the suicide of a relative, the funeral of a baby brother. It takes time to recreate the death-style in your family home, the folk wisdom, the religious answers, the fears, the silence and the reaction to tragedy. If you are patient and persistent, your actual feelings may float to the surface. Maybe you will find you are less fearful or uneasy than you thought. Assuredly you can find the source of your reluctance to visit dying friends, to attend funerals or to call on the bereaved.

Let me reassure you it is okay to feel uneasy or afraid. It is okay to want to run, to send floral wreaths or mass cards instead of self. It is okay to feel eerie or unduly tense, to hide and cry, to want to swear or scream or lash out at easy targets. It is okay to feel relieved and even happy when someone dies. It is okay to feel whatever is real. Feelings have no morality. They are neither good nor bad, always ethically neutral.

Too long have we misinterpreted the ancient wisdom of saying nothing about the dead unless it is good. Properly interpreted, it means we ought not talk publicly about the private faults of the dead. If stymied, it is better to say nothing than to violate a trust of close association. Misinterpreted, this adage leads so many to deny their honest feelings about the dead in their past, either privately to themselves or confidentially to a trusted friend. Maybe you loved your parents but secretly resented them for dying when or how they did. It is okay to face that fact as you reflect and to own the feelings it generates. It is also okay to talk about your "odd" feelings with a friend.

Few human relationships can ever be characterized as

exclusively bonds of love and fondness. Our ties to each other are far more complex. Often love coexists with fierce hate, and rage commingles with the deepest warmth. Violent emotions of every kind can be locked in hearts too frightened to find out how they truly feel about dying.

It takes time and tiring work to unearth the untouched feelings in our past. The promise is worth the effort. At the other end of the emotional gauntlet lies the art of graciousness near death, the personal freedom to die in peace and dignity, to help others die the same and to comfort grieving friends with more than sympathy cards and contributions to their favorite fund. I hope you can accept the challenge.

# 3.
# Fear of Death
# Is Fear of Life

"Talk is cheap. It takes money to buy whiskey." So spoke my dear Irish grandmother whenever she disbelieved a sincere friend. After interviewing hundreds of people concerning their death-related fears, I discovered how terribly expensive whiskey must be.

Who can you believe? Interviewees whose haughty denials of fear come out in nervous haste, muffled voices or loud protestations? Those who vow indifference but will not change the subject? Or those who talk "machismo" talk like they tell the speed of their Porsche or their sexual prowess? Take any of these brave denyers to a deathbed or a morgue and their facades crumble. Voices falter, palms grow damp and they manufacture wild excuses to hurry away. Claims of fearlessness around human mortality are often no more than inexpensive talk.

I finally decided to listen carefully and credibly to a lovely woman speaking from the other side of most death fears. After months of dying she was only weeks from death when we met. Elaine's fears are typical, but her courage and solutions are not. In the prime of life, she remembered herself as fearless, until the doctor announced her fate and the fear of hearing his words was the beginning fear in her litany.

After much encouragement and persuasion, Elaine agreed to the use of her thoughts anonymously. She wanted her family to have more than the legend of her fears in memory. Later she confided that her initial reluctance was a fear her ideas would prove useless and she would be rejected in her dying need to reach safely out to people. I assembled the interview from tape recordings, notes and phone calls, using all of her ideas with many of my words. Elaine edited and approved the interview three weeks before she died.

Quiet and reflective reading is suggested. So much of what Elaine confides could come from any dying lips that friends would loosen. I found many of her fears hidden behind unique defenses in my own daily life. Elaine claimed she learned too late how much lessons learned near death would prove valuable in life. I am happy Elaine learned at least when she did.

### Elaine's Story

I am thirty-seven and for the first time in my adult life I am not ashamed to reveal my true age. It takes the edge off all the years I'll never have, to brag about the ones I had. The doctor has not set a final date though I sometimes wish he would. It would be easier, like going into surgery on schedule. I only know I will not keep my date for a thirty-eighth birthday party with Arnold and our daughters.

I am not too frightened anymore. In fact, I am accepting, even resigned. If you want total frankness, the whole rigamarole of dying has become an irking bore. Two doctors stop by irregularly to check my comfort level and push their pills. My minister came almost every day until I foolishly told him I thought I was falling in love with him. Now he comes about twice a week when Arnold is here and reads or prays for me. I suppose he is too uncomfortable to deal personally with me, probably afraid I will cause a scene. The nurses are super to me, almost too perfect in answering every need. I'd feel better if somebody around here would goof so I could crab and complain. It certainly would be more like the real me.

Arnold comes every evening and spends most of every weekend around the hospital. Strangely, he seems to be mourning me early, missing me before I'm gone or maybe getting ready to be a widower. All our affairs are talked out and tears were turned off months ago, so we engage in small talk or sit silently for hours. The poor guy seems so tired of all my suffering and dying. I cannot blame him. So am I. Dying drags. You feel almost prepared to go and nothing happens, you start getting ready all over again.

Arnold brings the girls twice a week, always scrubbed and prettied, but it hurts and I feel myself withdrawing from them. I cannot tell whether I only want to miss them gradually or if it is because they represent life and that world out there with kitchens and schools and laughter. Nobody ever laughs around me. Our bridge gang comes occasionally to kibbitz about old times and to pretend that another few Saturdays will mean another rubber. Drifters wander in and out, friends overcome by kindness or guilt. Their presence causes me to feel they would never come at all if they had not promised to come when they called or dropped a note.

Never in my life have I felt more alone. An opportunity to share my thoughts brings new purpose into my day. My original reluctance was only because I wanted to be begged, since I was afraid my willingness would make you think I was too anxious and maybe you'd find somebody more thoughtful. I used to measure days by meals and visiting hours and nights by pills and shots, but time flies now as I reflect on what you asked. What were my fears about dying and death? How did I handle them? What are they still?

Funny, before my surgery for breast cancer, I pictured myself as another Joan of Arc. I was fearless. I knew little about death and cared less. It was never discussed in my family home or in my own house. I was about nine when Aunt Marge died at eighty-seven and death seemed so normal. I never went close when relatives or neighbors died, always found an excuse. Death seemed as unreal to me as space travel did when I used to read Buck Rogers in the funnies. Now I feel like an astronaut, about to go but not too well prepared.

Please don't laugh at my first reactions when I knew I was going to die. I read every book I could find on the fear of death and was determined my fears would disappear if I could understand their origins. I was turned off by the ideas of Freud. He said people have no fear of death in their unconscious mind, but all death fears are rooted in our fear of being castrated. I could better believe his critics who felt men fear the loss of the entire self in death far more than the mere loss of sexuality in castration.

I read dozens of theories, far-out ones, like the psychologists who say death-related fears are the reverse side of our feelings of omnipotence in youth. Well-loved children develop a sense of being all-powerful, even in their wishes. In anger they might tell someone to "drop dead" or wish secretly they would go away for good. Later, when such persons die or disappear, the youngsters tremble in their power and guilt overwhelms them.

These theories rang no bells for me. I found a better fit for my feelings and experience in psychologists who saw death fears as our organism's natural resistance to dying or not being. This made death seem to unify all of nature in one grand reluctance to abandon life. I could see plants in my garden struggling to live and unwilling to die. Our sixteen-year-old dog seemed to die each time he slept, only to wake and eat voraciously, then seem to die again. Most of all I remembered those awful sow bugs in their annual invasion of my shower. Bare feet were never enough when they cuddled to ward off death. It took a shower slipper to stop them.

I found this same resistance to death in myself. Unlike dogs and sow bugs, I knew the future and understood the risks in living. I knew cancer was threatening me and I was apprehensive of the pain in dying. From this awareness, I believe most of my fears were born. Even when I thought I had discovered the origins and roots of my fears, they did not dwindle much and only a few minor ones disappeared. I knew I needed other ways to fight besides the handfuls of tranquilizers I was gulping every day.

My minister suggested I stop dodging and face my fears squarely. At the outset, all of them were jumbled together in one big lump inside. As courage came, I could sort and identify, going with each fear wherever it would lead. Not one of them was as painful as all the panic I first felt in running to escape them.

For hours I would stay quietly alone, purposely, tasting my fears, letting them rummage freely inside, until I learned that even fear has a built-in dissipater. So much original panic ebbed away. At times I dared do or say things I feared the most and that helped more than anything. I was reluctant to know the full truth of my condition but I pumped the doctor until he blurted everything he knew. Almost miraculously, as

I worked, alternately allowing my fears and attacking them, so many drifted away, and all were less frightening.

Maybe it would help if I shared my major fears and how I stumbled through them. As I look back and forward, I find my worst fears were grouped in four clusters—around the process of dying, my actual death, the idea of afterlife and the entire abysmal aura that hovers around the dying.

Way back, my apprehensions centered around my images of what dying would be like. I think television had conditioned my mind to expect unbearable agony and I was especially terrified of pain. Shortly I learned the wisdom of Freud's observation that pain is experienced to the extent that the mind remains inactive or unengaged. People around me would fret when I fractured their classic image of what a dying patient should be and insisted on doing something important or responsible. They all seemed badly in need of my sitting there dolefully or lying there, waiting. The less I was needed, the more I needed drugs.

It took time to help my family and friends through the gimmick stage. Crossword puzzles, jigsaws, nightly card games. Monopoly with the girls, etching, painting and macramé, all things I disliked and only did to make others feel rewarded in my proper activity. My contentment was in theirs and that worked fine for a while, but who wants an eternity of fun and games? The more Arnold and I could discuss our affairs and the more responsible tasks he left for me, the more creative and worthwhile I felt. Reading everything you always wanted to read was fun, until you could. I needed some direction.

Would you believe I started studying for the real estate salesman's license? My ceaseless reading was almost as thrilling as Arnold's nightly examinations. It took five weeks and I needed special permission to leave the examining room three times, but I passed with an 84. I was searching for my first real job while I was dying. A broker friend agreed to hang my license in his office and on my rare good days I tried a turn at office duty. It was no good so I worked at home by phone, mostly soliciting new listings. With Arnold's help, I sold two houses and my mind was forever whirring with offers, deals, figures and ads. Even as late as two weeks ago I took a new listing and whenever the pain becomes too much, I still find myself wheeling and dealing, putting packages or deals together for imaginary customers. If they sell the house I listed before I die, I told Arnold I could afford my own funeral. Staying useful and important has been my best antidote for pain.

Maybe it's unwise to share my cute secret, but what has a dying woman got to lose? After I switched to a new medicine, my stomach was constantly nauseated with horrible wretching. My doctor winkingly told how some patients found relief in smoking marijuana and suggested we might try some. I will never forget the look on Arnold's face, petrified when he left, radiant when he returned in triumph. Some kids accused him of being a narc and refused to sell. One rascal chided him to grow up and drink. With a few drags on a joint the nausea disappeared, so Arnold kept going.

Whenever I needed to take another trip, Arnold acted like a criminal. He would shoo the girls, pull the drapes and lock every door. Then he played policeman until the odor was completely gone. After reading about how LSD had helped patients at Johns Hopkins hospital, I begged Arnold to get me a dose but the doctor refused to experiment. I think Arnold was relieved because he thought for sure heroin would be next. I still wish I had been able to try acid but most of my fears are quiet without it.

Once you live long enough with pain you forget what life

was like without it. Maybe you get used to it or maybe you simply lose all terms of comparison except to rejoice that this minute's pain is not as bad as last minute's. I keep finding little triumphs that cloud out what being free from pain would mean.

Dying also frightened me because I would become a burden to others. I was an independent cuss, the doer in our house, the giver on our block. I never learned the art of receiving graciously. I was forever returning two dozen cookies on a plate that arrived with only one. As my strength receded, I could picture myself being lifted, washed, fed, turned, even toileted, tying everyone I loved to the growing burden of my needs. Jealousy flourished as I watched Arnold come and go and the girls being so carefree, until resentment made me mean enough to act more helpless than I was.

I never dreamed how much the helpless could offer others from a sickbed. I forced myself to ask for things and learned to swallow my shame. I cannot tell you how thrilling it was to learn new ways to express my love. Arnold and I mastered a totally new style of cooperative love as he lifted me in and out of the bathtub, on and off the bathroom stool, laughing, struggling together like when we were first married, grunting, totally oblivious of time, sometimes collapsing in hysterical laughter when we slipped or when we needed to pause for breath. Arnold often whispered how excitingly sexual this new way of sharing love could be and I knew what he meant as I clung to him in the abandon of utter helplessness. Sexual intercourse was no longer possible for me, but it surely made a girl feel good to know she could still be sexual for her guy.

It was fun to watch the girls play mother, imitating my walk, my talk, my habits, feeding and nursing me, brushing my hair, remaking my bed. Arnold even bought them nurses' uniforms. Ginnie, my nine-year-old, would sit for hours doing my nails, while Cherrie, a firebug at only seven, would wait to light another cigarette. I smoked more than I ordinarily would and purposely scuffed my fingernails to insure their nearness.

My fear of being a burden has almost passed. Next to Arnold, my biggest help was Margie, a plump and shy eighteen-year-old from across the street. Margie has always had plans for the Peace Corps or for Vista but postponed any idea of helping the helpless overseas or in a ghetto to help one across the street. She would never accept a penny. She insisted that Arnold take the girls to a movie, then she would read to me, clean the house, do the laundry, organize my real estate doings, write my letters, and if time allowed, confide in me her deepest secrets. We grew to love and need each other in a wonderful way. I watched this bashful girl blossom in her new sense of purpose, and instead of feeling beholden, I learned to revel in my role as benefactor, knowing my burden had helped cultivate her new beauty. Never before had I helped anyone so much and enjoyed it so deeply. Margie told me so, too, when she tearfully announced her family had to move away.

The whole environment of dying arouses fears of indignity in a proud person whose cleanliness and modesty border on the neurotic. At times it was more than I thought I could bear. It was not too bad to spill food on fresh sheets or to clumsily drop ashes on a vacuumed floor. The rare times I contemplated suicide were when my bodily functions got out of control. Lying there in a puddle or a mess, too embarrassed to tell anyone what their nose already knew. When Arnold or Margie neared to freshen me, I pretended to be asleep, often wishing it were forever.

The depths of my indignity were unexpected. My main reactions were tearful, hysterical screaming jags reserved for hours when nobody was home. My willpower seemed to be separating from my body and my mind. No longer would my body respond and each new loss of function brought new shame and embarrassment. I could not turn or bend or slide. I could barely chew and turn my face. My sexual desires and excitation had long since mellowed, yet fantasies and dreams were filled with sexual scenes, often violent, and many a night I awakened while being raped. Pills and shots and other people took me over. I became in every sense a passive verb, from doing to done for, from is to was, from being to been. My basic pride and sense of decency tumbled in the full exposure of every human weakness.

Every mirror in the house reflected openly the tale of my indignity until Arnold took them all down. Then I could only imagine my appearance. Every visitor became a peeping tom, peeking at my falling hair, my sinking face, my peeling lips, my bleary eyes, my thinning yet bloated body.

I now know when and how and why I fell in love with my minister. He kept pointing to the rich and human beauty underneath my ghastly exterior. To a female who had long basked in the assurance that men found her attractive, it was exciting to listen to one who spoke of a charm and beauty beneath the disintegrating outer layer, of a feminine worth despite the insufferable odors and the disappearing breasts.

I began to find a rewarding kind of person-to-person intimacy beyond the purely physical. I understood for the first time how much of my sexual experience bypassed this intimacy between the spirits of two persons, leaping over the fear and tension of raw closeness and into only physical sex. It had always been easier to run away entirely or to perform physically, than to stay for any length of time with the intimacy I often felt but feared.

For long periods we would share this new perception of beauty and value in people too scarred or too deformed to make any mark in a society that rejected physical defects as harshly as the people who had them. I learned to identify with every overweight woman I had ever known. Too late my eyes could see beauty beneath acne and frizzy hair, behind birthmarks and pimple breasts. I understand and forgive my pastor's flight. How would his wife and congregation relate to an affair with a dying Magdalene? Besides, healthy bodies probably cannot take the pressure and passion of such overwhelming intimacy like sick bodies can.

Now I am not ashamed when visitors come and I can even comfort them when they muff their lines or dare not look my way. Mirrors hold no terror now, and I asked Arnold to rehang every one on my last visit home. Visitors tell of an inner beauty reflected in recent smiles. I feel it, too, and know mirrors inside are reflecting images never seen before. I am sorry I found these inner mirrors too late to help my girls find theirs. Instead of the indignity I feared, I now feel human love can deepen in nakedness, if pride disappears. My indignity was lost in the dignity of loving hands and in the power of eyes retrained to see within.

Looking in my rear-view mirror, the fears of dying were the easiest to face, but I suppose every fear seems simple after you win. I am still afraid of what I will lose in being dead. All mastery over yourself is gone, all control. This is my first fear in actual death, but not my worst. I never realized until now what a controlling person I have been and how important it was to manipulate people and situations. Dying helps in letting go of this need to control, but when death actually comes, even my mind, my thoughts and memories will go. I keep comparing this fear to the feeling I had the only New Year's Eve I got drunk. I teetered on the brink of consciousness, fearful that in letting go I would lose my whole self.

Arnold and the girls suffered much from the strings of guilt my martyrdom and bitching put on them. Our house was like a puppet show with Elaine as puppeteer. It would be nice to go home without needing to be on top, in charge of everything. The less I need to manipulate the more I can accept and love my family.

A second fear that death itself introduces is one of separation and all it implies. All my loves will be gone, but more than that, I will be replaced by new loves, maybe better ones. Arnold may marry again and the girls will have another mother. Every important relationship will be severed at once, and I cannot imagine any replacement. More than people are involved. My china, my roses, my silver tea set, my antiques, my favorite dress—all petty losses if you can get replacements, but major if you are going away for good.

My identity is so defined by my roles, I wonder who I will be when the girls wave goodbye, when Arnold plants his final kiss, when Mom and Dad come from Hawaii for their final hug. No longer mother, no longer wife, no longer anybody's daughter. *Former* everything: former leader to the girl scouts, a former member at my church; even the hospital will take me off their list. For two days I will find identity in the obituaries, and then what will I be besides a memory?

Near the end, casual acquaintances like nursing aides and cleaning ladies become important. I feel closer to the children of Mrs. Paulson in the next bed than to most of my friends. The kids are always here and they treat me like their mother's neighbor instead of like a dying cancer patient. X-ray technicians and some grey ladies are closer than relatives. And little things become monumental, like when I visit home for a few days, the ring of the mailman, the "clump" of the paper on the porch and the tinkle of the ice cream truck, all become major events in my evaporating world. Soon even these will be gone. I keep wondering who I will be when no familiar sounds can be heard, when no label fits, not even that lady in 329, bed A.

I am surprised my faith did not help more in dulling the fear of separation. I always planned on meeting God but was forever baffled by whether He might look like Christ or a bearded father. When my believing self is plugged in, I still expect to meet angels and saints, but to meet spirits is hardly exciting and to make so many new friends is unattractive when I'd rather keep the ones I have.

Another fear in actual death is at the incompleteness of my life. I can recite my failures and my omissions better than my harshest critic, since even trifles pass through my mind continually. It seems normal to mourn what dead children might have done, but I'm no child, I had my chance. Still I mourn the lacks left in my marriage, the unfinished task of rearing my girls, my home decorated far below my aspirations and my hours of charitable work that lie ahead. The incompleteness of little things bothers me most, like the yellow and green dresses I started for my majorettes.

I cannot define satisfactorily a time when I might not feel my life were incomplete. If God offered me ten more years I would hold out for fifteen. I want to see the girls through grade school and counsel them through puberty. I want to fly with Arnold when he completes the lessons he gave up to pay for my surgery. I have an insatiable appetite for doing more and seeing everything, so I am repeatedly aware of the road ahead that I will never travel.

When you asked for my reflections on death fears, I was working on my fears connected with afterlife. A number of my present anxieties seem rooted in where I will be when the doctor says I'm gone. I am ashamed to admit I worry a lot about what will happen to my body, even though it looks pretty awful now. I cannot stop thinking that some part of me will be watching my funeral, looking out from the casket-counting mourners, still living somehow in that cemetery grave beneath a monument. Decay and cremation repulse me for the same reason. I'll be there. Before surgery, science could easily have had my body, but now I say to everybody: "Leave my body alone!" The poor thing has been tampered with enough and deserves some rest. What I really fear in my anger is they will be cutting up Elaine.

I used to believe all believers in cryonics were crazy. How could anyone pay ten thousand dollars to remain frozen in a jar until they find a cure for cancer and men are kind enough to open up the jar? Now, if we had the money, I might join those "crazies." I want to live even though I am resigned to die. Life in a jar seems more appropriate than decay and claustrophobia in a grave and less painful than crematory fires. Wherever my body lies, there am I, and no matter how illogical, I cannot divest myself of this thought, nor can I long for any other kind of life.

It seems paradoxical that I cannot conceive of the departure of my soul from my body—while some days I fear my soul will burn in hell. From childhood in the Baptist faith, I related more to hell than to heaven. Maybe because there is so much guilt in me, such a sense of unworthiness. My minister would only talk of heaven while childhood ministers filled my head and heart with fear of fire and brimstone. The hopeful Bible quotes I now hear twice a week seem like a eulogy in advance. It has been so many years since I talked to anyone who took hell seriously, in fairness, I almost wish one of those fiery preachers from my past would reappear. Maybe then I would know if I am being mollycoddled by modern religion. Now I cannot tell whether my apprehension is the echo of a frightened past or the tug of a conscience so steeped in sin and worldliness it cannot feel forgiven.

Can you believe the happiness of heaven seems almost as fearfully strange as the fires of hell? It seems naive to talk of clouds and palatial mansions when I have acrophobia and will have no body to sit on the throne. Fire is real, but every image used to describe heaven seems foreign when all you want is homemade bread and plum jam, a chance to dance and laugh again, some time to putter in your yard. When religious visitors ask, I do violence to the truth and tell them I am prepared, even happy to go to a heaven that frightens me. Life is too short to make them unhappy.

I used to shudder at the thought of eternal sleep but now it suits me fine. Too much sleep always seemed like squandering life until lately. After months of groggy days and fitful nights, I am not afraid to drift off, though I wonder if the real Elaine is talking or only my pain and need for some unbroken rest.

I think my faith attracted me in life because I never liked loose ends, riddles or ambiguity. I like things well defined and too many "maybes" upset me. I sometimes feel I believed too hard and drove my mind past all other possible beliefs without taking a good look at any but my Baptist background.

Maybe I will be a peasant in France or a St. Bernard dog in the Alps. Or maybe I'll reincarnate into an angel. I could become a spook wandering hauntingly about, talking to Arnold through a medium or following the girls on Halloween. It seems absurd, but I may well go to purgatory and long for masses most of my friends do not believe in. If I have enough time, I want to read more, since this is my most pressing anxiety. Where will Elaine be after death?

A fourth area of fear permeated the entire dying scene. I

cannot completely sort them out or pinpoint them, but they are rumbling inside and I want to be honest. Liars go to hell, you know.

As I declined physically, an aura of hopelessness descended around me, the most fearful atmosphere I ever faced. It was terrifying. Nothing within prepared me to cope with it effectively without being cruel. Mine has been an optimistic view of life, so to date, my only cure for hopelessness has been in being my own cheerleader, leading myself in phony pep talks that I loathe when others use them on me. "Come on, Elaine, think positive, chin up, be brave, you are only as old as you feel!" I tell myself to be grateful for my memories, my family and that I didn't die at thirty-two instead of thirty-seven. Ickiness! If I were not so ill already, this would make me sick. I often wish Arnold would walk in, the Arnold of old, and tell me some dirty jokes so we could laugh.

Blaming others for your feelings is foolish, yet I find myself resenting callers with doleful faces. They look like undertakers are supposed to look. I want to shout out: "Hey, damn you, take that look off your face, it's me that's dying!" I cannot expect them to smile or joke, but I would feel like hugging and kissing the first one who did.

The entire hospital smacks of hopelessness once the secret of your doom spreads down the corridors, in and out of rooms, on elevators, in radiology, in the kitchen and through changing shifts. I fear the whispering around me, the sadness etched on faces and the babying approach everyone assumes. Voices change pitch and tone when directed toward you. You feel cut off and marked like a contagious leper. I watched them do it to the lady in the room with me and then to me.

Another fear I cannot describe adequately is my growing horror of being rejected by anyone. I feel a need to be overly kind and agreeable, to put up with guff from anyone, always saying "yes" when the answer is really "no." I want to be alone and yet I need people near me. Maybe you can understand better if you know how blurred the mind becomes after long confinement and tons of drugs. You believe you are as ready to die as time and talents permit, yet a single rejection from a janitor could convince your tired mind that you are not prepared at all. You fear that in a single rejection you might know that all your efforts to die peacefully were a cruel hoax perpetrated upon yourself to avoid the reality of death. Any hint of rejection intensifies my fear of dying alone, abandoned, isolated and in terror.

I guess if I am totally honest, I also fear my thoughts will not be of any help. If you do find your death fears nestled next to mine, I can assure you they are not as fearful as I anticipated. If your fears are of another kind, I wish you luck in pioneering. I sometimes get an urge to shoot or at least soundly spank all who taught me fear was evil and somehow less than human.

I found the endless running and worrying far more painful than my fears. I learned much and am trying to learn until I cannot. Most important, I found that those around me who were not busy running from their fears could be my closest and only effective friends as death came near. Once we shared our fears, we found how many were groundless, and the realistic ones lost much sting in our sharing and mutual helpfulness.

I wish someone had told me that the only impossible fear is the fear to feel and share your feelings with others. Those who love you can understand anything and all of us are stronger than any of us realize. I think my death will be almost happy, since my one pressing regret is that I cannot live to practice what I learned in dying.

# 4.
# Humane Treatment of the Terminally Ill

It was 2:12 p.m. on April 19 when Gabe entered the inner office. His appointment was for 1:30 p.m. and he had waited, as he expected, for Dr. Trapp, the king of overscheduling.

A perky, blond nurse, on the run, left him in a tiny examining room where the diploma on the wall and the paper-covered examining table exhausted his observations in a single glance. Again Gabe waited, this time alone with his thoughts, no magazines, no distractions, not even a window. He knew he was all right as he kept pinching and rolling the muscles in his lower abdomen, checking. The pain in his intestines had disappeared, all except a little.

Suddenly, at 2:34 p.m., Dr. Trapp entered the room, test results in hand. He plopped on the table and time meant nothing any longer.

Small talk galore. The young doctor shuffled and re-shuffled the papers, talking of a fishing trip to Mexico and of woodcarving, hoping to distract Gabe. There was no distracting. Gabe feigned interest in the trivia, straining to see the test results. Then it came.

"Our x-rays and tests reveal that your colon is considerably distended. This is due to an obstruction in the distal portion. The causes range from diverticulitis to carcinoma. We have made arrangements for you to check into Parks Memorial Hospital tonight before nine and surgery will be early tomorrow morning. Dr. Reggs will perform the surgery and I will scrub in."

(The doctor kept talking, though he might well have stopped at carcinoma. Polyps, adhesions, volvulus interspersed with polysyllabic words Gabe neither understood nor remembered.) Blah! Blah! Blah! Gave felt like leaping to the examining table and bellowing the loudest blasphemy or the filthiest words in his limited vocabulary. His mind and ears turned off. His body ached for the touch of a hand, an arm around his shoulders, a warm and reasuring ! ug. Now Dr. Trapp stood his distance behind the examining table, unwilling to offer even a straightforward look. Gabe wanted trivia, funny talk, anything but the jargon that overwhelmed him until he could not . . . would not . . . listen.

What to tell Helen? Who will break in the new secretary at the office? Will this mean an end to sex for good? Should I tell the children? How will my parents take it? Gabe wanted to ask the doctor for a belt of bourbon. It might help him step away a bit, gain some distance, maybe cry a little.

Gabe's head began to reel with crying people, fearful stares, white-coated doctors, puttering nurses, scalpels, bed pans, needles, squishy food and bandages. Nausea came when he imagined that hospital smell and the silence. Already he felt himself missing friends who were sure to stay away from cancer. Is it contagious? Is it always fatal? Will I have treatment burns all over me? Will insurance cover? Will I die? How long?

Dr. Trapp was still talking, still answering questions Gabe had not asked, drawing profound medical analogies while looking from floor to ceiling with an occasional side glance at Gabe. Gabe felt like any patient, no warm vibrations of uniqueness, or of even being special, like any caller from the Yellow Pages under "Physician." He wanted to ask questions he did not want answered. He wanted to slam doors and shake his fist at heaven, but instead, Gabe the "nice guy" took over, sitting controlled and with fixed face while his medical eulogy droned on.

Then Gabe was outside and in his car. Twice on the journey home, he pulled along the curb to gain composure. At first he fought back his feelings, bawled himself out for acting like a baby, then he blubbered like one, totally out of control. He wondered if he could face an entire evening of pretending without any answers. Nobody would know his fears. Helen had enough on her mind with a home and four children. The children were too young to know anything of death and carcinoma. People at the office would gossip and speculate on their next manager. Mom and Dad were too old and far away. Aunt Maude would only break down. There was nobody else to tell, yet something inside kept insisting that he call everybody so the world would come to him in pity and hugging consolation.

Gabe bluffed through the news and almost through supper. Helen noticed him toying with his favorite pot roast and browned potatoes and when she caught him laughing too loud, he whispered to her of his hospital appointment, biting her ear in levity. The youngsters bickered and tussled as usual, looking for Scotch Tape and ballpoints, crying for a referee, blaming with "See what you made me do!" Gabe savored each little scene, sipping his burgundy and coffee. It might be his last night at home.

Gabe carefully kissed each little face goodnight. They were too old to volunteer but young enough not to resist his buss. Not one of them noticed his special care or resisted his longer hug. When they were alone, Helen began her hovering, begging for answers without details, laughing without humor, touching him with no feeling, filling his wine glass before it was empty, looking at him, but seeing something far beyond. Gabe shared none of his misgivings, telling as little as Helen would accept. She seemed like a stranger and he imagined himself a prisoner sentenced to death.

Gabe vetoed Helen's plan to drive him to the hospital, and now as the cab wound through traffic he alternately prayed and bargained with God. "My God, why me?" Long ago he had cooled on prayer and Sunday Mass. Now he wondered if this could be a sign from on high. He worked out a deal for his Maker: no cancer, no missing Mass. He pictured Helen telling the children, sending them off to school with a better lunch than usual. She would fabricate a white lie for the boss. He felt at peace as he walked up the steps—Helen, the children, the boss and God were taken care of, all on his side.

Gabe signed himself in and a friendly nurse led him to his room where his elderly roommate lay moaning softly. In bed and quiet, he unconsciously reached for Helen, somehow relieved not to find her. Thermometer, shaving, a needle, pills and sleep. Next morning he could hardly remember being whisked away but could recall Dr. Trapp standing over him in his funny hat. Then nothing until a shadowy Helen leaned over him, tired and worried. He touched her hand and she smiled.

No doctor, only nurses gliding in and out of his vision. Helen everywhere, water and grease for his lips, patting his brow, fluffing the pillow, straightening his sheets. She looked like a little girl on Halloween, frightened in her costume of an old lady. Any minute he expected her to say: "Trick or treat!"

Gabe took her hand and asked for his doctor. Helen pushed a button. Only nurses came to parry. "Dr. Trapp will be along, you understand how busy the poor man is." Gabe tried to understand, drifting sleepily, waking again to see his little girl looking as if she had changed seasons. Now Helen looked like she knew there was no Santa Claus but dared not tell.

Time was measured in worries. No hours or minutes, only Helen and kids, job and unemployment coverage, savings and insurance, parents and talkative neighbors, his tropical fish and God. Dr. Trapp appeared, smiling at the foot of the bed, fondling his pen and fumbling with a chart, checking needles and bottles at a glance. Staring at someone behind Gabe, he pronounced the solemn words of medical absolution: "Well, old man, I think we got it all!"

Gabe's relief was immediate if short-lived. Was this a bogus pardon? Am I getting the full story? Even Marcus Welby hedged at times. Does Helen know a separate version of my story or is she only tired?

Gabe's face told the discomfort of his doubts and Helen moved to the doctor's rescue. "Honey, all of us are so grateful and happy. The children are fine and send their love, they miss you and want you home real soon. They begged to come after school but you know hospital rules. Father Kinton happened by while you were sleeping and said he only wanted to cheer you up. He left a special blessing right from Pope Paul himself. Your folks called to see how you are and Aunt Maude called, too. Your office sent these beautiful flowers and the boss delivered this beautiful card signed by all. . . ."

At some place in the rescue mission Dr. Trapp exited

smilingly, waving without a word. Helen, poor Helen, only sputtered on.

Gabe had always been fond of playing games. Now that his life was at stake, his likes changed. After eleven long days of ignorance in the hospital and ten more at home, with Helen and Dr. Trapp making and enforcing rules, Gabe gladly went back to the office. This was a no-win game.

Folks around the office appeared a trifle too happy to have him back. Nobody inquired about his health, preferring to tell him how well he looked in tones and phrases allowing for no reply. The boss offered a small raise. "Nothing like a little sickness to make us realize who is really important around here, Gabe!" The new secretary, already well-trained, volunteered for after hours to clear his desk. The gang begged for lunches where martinis kept conversation light. Gabe could not drink and could only feign conviviality, too intense in wondering.

Now the children found their own Scotch Tape or went without. Seldom any bickering or forgetting to kiss daddy without a reminder. Helen encouraged more lovemaking than even a healthy Gabe could handle. Every night she seemed ready, usually anxious. Favorite dishes every night at supper. Twice Father Kinton came. Both times Helen waved the men into the living room for man-talk over Drambuie and coffee. Aunt Maude wrote a long letter and Gabe knew he was a dying man.

Should patients who are doomed to die know their fate? This used to be a troublesome question, the most baffling in the entire issue of dying. Discussions were always theoretical. No scientific or clinical evidence existed for the comparison of the benefits in telling the patient with the benefits of remaining silent. Everybody guessed. Parlor talk and religion classes abounded with moral platitudes about man's right to know his condition or about our duty to keep the patient comfortable by silence. "Every man has the right to know so he can put his house in order!" "Happiness is an inalienable right and should not be destroyed when nothing is accomplished!" Doctors differed in theory. In practice they were nearly unanimous in not telling. Clergymen leaned toward telling, though were easily convinced otherwise if they were asked to tell. The dying were seldom consulted, only left to suffer the results of the arguments outside their door.

At last we have abundant clinical evidence on what happens when dying patients are told their fate. And by deduction, we know what happens when they remain ignorant. Almost without exception, the case histories reveal the value of an early and forthright disclosure. Dr. Elisabeth Kubler-Ross, the best known of the researchers, clearly documents the several stages which dying people pass through. From an original posture of denial and isolation, patients made aware of their terminal condition pass through stages of anger, bargaining, depression and acceptance or resignation, without ever fully losing hope. Her documentation scuttles all our traditional arguments for reluctance. Patients who know their destiny can progress toward a peaceful and dignified death. Those left in ignorance of their diagnosis rarely make it past the fearful stage of denial and isolation.

In yesterday's speculation and confusion, the line of least resistance always became most attractive. Since patients were not asked, it was the teller's resistance that was measured. It was much simpler not to tell. Now we know it was not so easy for the untold patients.

Today, we can say with certainty that as a general rule, every patient should be made aware of his diagnosis. There may be exceptions, but I hesitate to mention a single one, because the fearful will find their own excuse in any exception I select. Instead of listing exceptional situations, I prefer to say that the only remaining questions are clear. When should the patient be told? How should he be told? And who should do the telling?

The terminal patient should know his prognosis as soon as it is medically certain. Any disclosure to any patient, most especially an early one, needs to be padded in hope. Doctors have been in error and predictions can be faulty. There have been sudden and near miraculous changes in conditions. New developments in medicine and in surgery are always around the corner.

Human beings have a magnificent filtering system built into their perceptual senses. When discussing any delicate subject, this system sifts out any data the mind is not ready to know. No matter how loud, how clear or how often the speaker communicates an unwanted fact, the human mind resists acceptance until it is ready. You see this filtering system at work when lovers spat. The rejected lover always hears in hope, no matter how final the rejector makes his case. You can see this filter at its comic best in middle-aged marrieds who grow conveniently deaf to each other's bickering, while capable of hearing outsiders with ease. The dying make use of this remarkable system, filtering out what they will not know or are not ready to realize. Or, they listen now and hear later on, when facts can be digested at their individual pace and emotions are prepared to react to truth.

When death comes quickly and the dying person has only hours or days, it is still a general rule that the patient prospers by knowing what is taking place. In telescoped form, they endure the same problems and can move through the same stages as the lingering. They, too, will filter out what they would not not know. The shock and tension around sudden deaths are usually so great that any rules I might offer would be pure folly. Bystanders need only try to do their best, not copping out to their personal fears and natural reluctance while the patient dies uninformed in hysteria and terror. Even a little talking, a little listening, coupled with loads of straightforward looking, eye to eye, will bring significant comfort and relief.

Heart patients, whose need to avoid additional stress is uppermost in every bystander's mind, need special consideration. The very act of telling about impending death is feared to cause it. Such victims need to talk, or if talking is no longer possible, they need to emote in any way they can, as long as consciousness lasts. They need human presence, with hands to hold and eyes that dare answer lovingly the questions their own eyes ask. They need loving listeners and lookers who understand that minimal talking, even wordless speech with eyes and hands, can alleviate much of the terror a sudden confrontation with death can bring.

There is no easy way to tell another human being that death is near. Awkwardness can be expected. Fear and uneasiness are always partners to the telling, unless we have lost our normalcy or have callousness for a mask. It is always better by far if there is no act of telling at all—only a two-way conversation that is open enough to allow the patient to announce his dying if he chooses. Once we ask a patient how he feels, indicating in our asking that we truly want to know, usually we have said enough. Patients themselves will almost always introduce the subject of dying to permission-giving listeners. Most of the time, telling a person that he or she is dying means no more than chatting about the self, without nervous bandaids being put over the mouth or eager protestations of artificial hope.

Television has taught all of us to recognize deathbed scenes, and when we find ourselves bedded down in one, we make all necessary deductions. Our biggest need when we realize that death is coming is for a confidant who will instigate and allow our honest talk. So often when we hear of patients who did not want to know their terminal condition, we are actually hearing stories of relatives or bystanders who would not grant permission for candid conversation. A physician friend admitted that no patient of his had ever gone beyond the denial stage in dying, and he humbly knew that he was the major reason.

Patients who will not mention death when permitted to talk openly can be told in other ways. For literal folks, a medical diagnosis in straight terms might be the only way. For others, hints at being "terribly ill," of their being "sicker than ever before" or of our intense concern for their health, may do the trick. Such implications plant a seed from which the patient can make appropriate deductions in due time.

There are patients who want nothing more than to deny until the end, and our only need is to respect their right to know. When tellers are novices, there are no right or wrong ways. There are never any sure ways. There is only the ethical need that each patient knows the truth, as much as he wants and in a manner he can accept. Pushing human beings to know what they sincerely and inalterably wish to deny can be as inhumane as the universal silence of yesterday.

Who is the best person to inform the patient about a terminal condition? The doctor in charge of total patient care has the moral and professional responsibility to see that his patient knows. Many people are better equipped than the doctor for the actual telling. A son or a wife, a kindly nurse or a respected crony. There is no proper person, only one brave and humble enough to try bringing the maximum of graciousness to a forbidding task. Doctors who take into account the mental health of patients as part of their healing concern will see that every patient knows the truth as desired.

The physician in charge may be new to the case and believe the family physician a better choice. He may be a timid soul and need the support of a relative, a nurse or a chaplain. No longer can any physician pride himself as ethical and arbitrarily abrogate this responsibility with that flimsy excuse of bygone vintage: "Clinical experience dictates it is better for the patient not to know." Such clinical experience refers to a few trying experiences in early practice or cases borrowed from the lore of other equally frightened men. Clinical data is now clear and substantive enough to explode "old doctor tales" about the danger in telling the dying.

A major barrier against open discussion of death is our lack of an American folk language in which all can communicate comfortably about every aspect of human mortality. "Terminal" and "cancer" are as real but as difficult to say out loud as penis and vagina were a few years back. Our tongue is devoid of household expressions and nonprofessional terms by which we can articulate our new and evolving attitudes toward human death. In our futility, we grasp at strands of the three professional vocabularies Americans are still compelled to use when speaking of death: the medical, the religious and the language of funeral directors.

The medical language specializes in words only fully understood by Greek scholars or by students preparing for an exam in medical school. Doctors themselves seldom comprehend their full meaning, for if they did they could easily translate them into terms others could understand. Of all professionals, doctors alone are granted the privilege to speak over the heads of their clients. The medical profession has not yet had its Vatican Council for reformation. Despite years of Latin and Greek, I feel like a little boy when my doctor prescribes or diagnoses.

Words in the medical language relate almost exclusively to the living organism and exclusively to the physical. Few words relate to man's feelings and almost none to his spiritual side. No wonder medics can appear so clumsy after a patient's death, devoid as they often are of practice and training, and without proper words for their feelings. The medical vocabulary speaks about the heart, not to it. But in respect for his dedicated skills and his promise of health, we allow the physician his evasion. He is spared the layman's feeling of nakedness near death.

The religious language is helpful to believers and vestigially valuable to nonbelievers. Catholics are surrounded in death talk from grade one, while other religious groups move more slowly. All of us display traces of religion in our death vocabulary. Believers take the words literally, while nonbelievers or partial believers rely on religious words for want of other terms.

Believers can sometimes seem cruel in forcing not only words but the beliefs they signify on the hapless dying. Many times I watched and sometimes cooperated as wives made last-ditch efforts to convert nonbelieving husbands. The husbands would repeat, ostensibly through God's grace, the exact words of a required creed, apparently accepting what the words implied. In retrospect, the husbands seemed more anxious to insure the loyalty and love of wives than in cherishing a new faith they had resisted as long as they had strength and freedom to do so.

Now, to hear religious people talk of death to nonbelievers sounds to me like bragging. Deathbed conversions seem more like a triumph in battle than a loving ministry to the needs of fearful men. It is more religious by any standard to touch heartfelt needs of the dying than to force words and beliefs on them in a final effort to make survivors appear as victors. I used to thrill at deathbed conversions. Now I wonder if I should not apologize to all those I helped convert when they were too weak and frightened to resist.

Morticians teach the rudiments of "funeralese" during the days surrounding a funeral. Like Parisians correcting American high school French, the morticians will rearrange every expression we attempt. How I remember being forced to learn or relearn this mortician's tongue for every wake or funeral! Ask where the "corpse" is and be told "Mr. Jones" or "the loved one" is in the Chapel of Eternal Peace. It takes an average family about a week to learn "funeralese" adequately, then they promptly forget it until death strikes again. For all the morticians and cemeterians in the land, even one with a major teaching university like Forest Lawn, where millions flock, have not been able to make this language a part of our folk tradition. And recently, more and more funeral directors have stopped trying.

Poetry and art forms depict death in esoteric or romantic terms, so do the psychological practitioners. Irish folkways and Italian mores have never made it into the mainstream of American tradition. We are badly in need of a universal folk language in which even common men can find expressions for their profound reactions near death. We need ways to tell of new attitudes toward the aging, of concerns in keeping human vegetables alive, of transplant donors and recipients, of relief at prolonged death, of staggering medical bills, of hesitations over funerals or mausoleums, and of dozens of other typically American problems our way of life involves. Such a folk language will provide expressions that speak of our sense of mystery, our perplexity, our pain and guilt, and of our distinctive awareness of loss.

No better argument could be provided for offering some death education courses in our upper schools than the hope of developing a folk language and some customs peculiar to our needs. If admitted to the schools, death could then be mentioned in our home, in polite parlors, until such talk would refine our customs and result in a folk language.

Doctors would be required to provide translations for their jargon, and funeral directors and clergy might learn our common language instead of forcing us to master theirs.

In his semiweekly visits, Gabe tried every trick imaginable to force Dr. Trapp into candor. Trapp insisted on remaining in tight control, forever reestablishing his position: "I think we got it all." Never a hint of what would happen if his thinking were mistaken. When Gabe begged, Trapp meandered into possible new drugs, new tests or consultation with a distant expert. Often Gabe saw his partner and could only engage in aimless nothings. More and more, the nurse remained in the office insuring against any gut-level conversation.

The social scene was equally as puzzling. Gabe could no longer tell friendly neighbors from anticipatory mourners. Flitting visits, cheery notes and homemade bread made honest friends hard to distinguish from anxious consolers. Every party seemed like a preview for his wake. People were forever adding extra jiggers to his drinks, embalming him in alcohol. Seldom would partygoers permit him to engage in a one-to-one conversation with anyone but Helen. Always an impersonal threesome, husbands rescuing wives, wives saving neighbors. At work, one secretary would always rescue another, a salesman would redeem the boss.

Gabe expected so much more of Helen. Under warm covers he tried to pour out his heart, begging tearfully to know the full story. He pleaded to know how long he had to live. Helen responded with rubs and hugs, finally resorting to Dr. Trapp's "I think we got it all!" until Gabe damned the words and forbade her ever to mention them again. She kept maneuvering Gabe into planning for tomorrow. Travel brochures littered the house and plans for their dream home were on the bedside table amidst the pills. When Helen could no longer rattle on, she tried enticing him into the silence of unfelt sex. Gabe hated silent sexuality as much as Helen hated his increasing tears.

Gabe tested Father Kinton. The first time they skirted death, but on the second visit, the Father told of a new book on heaven and how his own brother had delayed making a will until it was too late. When Gabe cornered him on religious grounds, demanding, Father Kinton took refuge in Dr. Trapp's forbidden words. And Gabe wondered if death made liars out of God's priests.

The confusion caused Gabe to wonder if he were losing his mind. Everywhere he saw signs of forthcoming death. Was he manufacturing them and reading them into words and situations? Most days he felt sane enough, but the scale documented that he was growing thinner. When he asked Dr. Trapp to recommend a psychiatrist he was told one was not necessary.

Since Helen and the children did his chores, Gabe idled many hours before an open book or an unseen television screen, sipping beer, rolling his stomach muscles to check for new pain. Over and over he selected his pallbearers, read his obituary and imagined his eulogy. More often he contemplated suicide as the threat of invalidism seemed more real.

Gabe was unable to pray. He went to Mass most Sundays as part of his bargain, but was not guilty when he missed, since he was unware if God had kept his part. At Mass his mind wandered to the center aisle where he could see his casket; grace before meals became only setting a good example for the children. He felt nobody was listening, on earth or in heaven.

Occasionally after work, Gabe sought honest conversation by stopping for a drink at a strange bar. Bartenders were allegedly the world's finest listeners. One night he dared open up to a warm bartender when suddenly the other end of the bar demanded much attention. Even ladies of uncomplicated virtue who were wont to pontificate on any subject excused themselves for the powder room when Gabe grew honest with them.

The pain in Gabe's abdomen intensified. No longer could he roll his muscles without wincing. When the constant pain brought nausea, he booked an unscheduled visit with Dr. Trapp. After tapping the area of soreness, with vast circumlocution, Dr. Trapp assured Gabe he was not losing his mind. He was dying.

Dr. Trapp looked everywhere but at Gabe as he explained how Helen had begged to engineer a few months of happiness for her family. "I went along for her sake. Never have I met anyone so insistent." No mention of his moral responsibility to his patient, nor even a hint at his own possible relief that Helen's insistence had allowed his evasion.

Four months to the day from his original surgery, Gabe underwent token surgery. "Nothing medical science can do, there's just too much!" Gabe felt strangely relieved when the doctor consoled him and when Helen lost her mask with four months of tears behind it. Gabe's grieving was nearly spent. He was far from happy but just as far from the need to be consoled for a loss he had lived with for many months. He realized his need for permission from Helen and Dr. Trapp, and until granted, he had a new role to play: consoler to survivors.

In a week, Gabe was home, working, and struggling to regain trust in Helen and his doctor. Family life moved on as usual. Helen wanted to continue the game with the children. Gabe refused. Together they discussed the when and how of telling. For hours they shared like rarely before, and each found an untapped reservoir in the other. Gabe felt that he was gradually receiving Helen's permission to die.

Once it becomes clear to a person that death is inevitable, two important problems need facing if death is to occur with any degree of serenity for all concerned. First, the dying person needs to receive permission to pass away from every important person he will leave behind. Only then can the patient begin to deal with his second problem, the need to voluntarily let go of every person and possession he holds dear. Both problems deserve careful consideration, since therein lies the crux of dignified and peaceful dying.

At first it might seem strange to insist that the dying need permission to do the inevitable. Isolated patients will have no significant others from whom to seek permission. The unfeeling and those living in loveless situations will assume their right to die, covering themselves with self-pity while maintaining an outward denial of what is happening. But patients who feel any degree of human closeness or of responsibility to others, who had love in their lives and people near who needed them, require permission if death is to be peaceful. There is no other way to still feelings of guilt for going, for copping out on life, for becoming an emotional and financial burden and for that feeling of horrible helplessness inside.

Reasonably sensitive persons know well and feel deeply the pain and sorrow their death will cause. They feel guiltily responsible even when they know logically they are not. Each tearstained face, each wringing hand, each look of futility, pushes buttons of guilt inside a patient who cares. Always before there was a way out of guilt, an apology or explanation, a promise not to fail again, an act of special kindness in reparation. Because when dying there is only a single and unacceptable solution, permission becomes essential.

Before any dying patient can know that he wants or needs to accept permission, the head needs to be cleared. Jealousy and resentment toward the living need first to be stilled. Self-pity needs to be reduced if not removed, and the masks of denial need lifting. All of this takes time and requires at times the services of an enduring friend like Helen.

Permission to die need never be spoken aloud or written. The patient can read his permission in the ability of each visitor to cope with him as a person. The patient readily understands that friends and relatives who refuse to visit or fail to confront him when they do, are blocking his death, refusing to let it become real. Visitors who grow hysterical or display an uncontrollable grief reveal to the patient strings of a dependency only someone harsh could violently sever.

Permission to die is granted in all open and honest confrontations where patient and visitor accept the reality and needs of each other. Together they willingly face the situation as it is. The patient reveals that he can die without displacing his feelings onto the living, blaming no one, demanding no beyond-the-grave commitments. The visitor, in turn, displays his ability to keep living without blaming the patient, without threatening irremediable anguish. Doctors and nurses grant their permission by continuing regular and devoted care when comfort replaces recovery as the plan of patient care. Occasional friends grant their permission by a continued availability without losing respect for the patient's recurring need for privacy.

Clinical studies record a visible relief in patients when loved ones accept their dying without blame or despair. Other patients seem to survive beyond usual expectations, suffering ineffable pain, as if waiting like beggars for a "yes" from important people. After administering the last rites, I frequently noted a new sense of relief in the patient. Naturally, I advertised the worth of the sacrament. Now, I wonder if the reception of the sacrament was not the patient's assurance that everyone important had given permission.

Helen was a rare wife. Once the pretension game was over, she understood how a part of her would die in Gabe and she struggled to allow it. Gabe knew that in Helen's acceptance of his death, there was a kernel of acceptance from his children, his parents, his doctors and his friends. As the most important person in his life, her resignation and acceptance would model similar attitudes in others. Nobody had more to lose than Helen, except Gabe himself.

At times Helen expressed the resentment she felt toward Gabe for his departure, leaving her alone with four children and too many bills. She had no profession and had never had a real job, so she was afraid. At times her jealousy made her wish she were going away instead, if not so finally. As Helen shared her ignoble thoughts, Gabe knew she would not renege.

Several times daily Gabe calculated his net financial worth. Little enough for staples, nothing toward luxuries or college. He knew well the plans he was scuttling, the opportunities that would die with him, the gaping wounds his death would leave in five hearts. He knew his unfinished dreams and tasks. His deepest pain was in his inability to alter his lot a trifle. He found himself now bypassing pain pills to save pennies. Helen's dogged willingness to hear him out, to accept his guilt, to allow his worries without instant answers and to take up the family struggle alone, all eased his abiding sense of impotence.

Once the permission to die is clearly granted, the dying

patient can tackle the second major task, his personal work in voluntarily letting go. He can begin to release his hold on life, then gently, with growing decisiveness, unlock the chains that bind his heart to all earthly treasures, to valued persons and to every possession. He begins with the outer circle of important acquaintances and business associates now rarely seen, extending to close friends and family. His individual freedom grows as he releases job and future plans, favorite scenes, golf clubs, yard and home. If there is to be a tranquillity near death, all the dying can retain are what they truly own: their minds and loves, their memories and freedom, and their faith.

What does it mean to let go? Internally, the dying individual agrees to allow the world to go on without him. Positively put, he clings feverishly to all that is truly his own, learning to revel in himself and in his personal treasures. He learns to rejoice in what he is and has, ceasing to play Silas Marner with spouse and children, income and estate. At birth as at death, man is alone. At birth, our aloneness can only be felt in primitive feelings, while at death, our early feelings are resurrected and we know our isolation. The human struggle for the dying is not so much in letting go as in reaching out for revelry in what we hid from ourselves in life.

Once the terminal patient begins to unleash himself from ties and roles, he increasingly becomes a free spirit. His survivors also gain new freedom in his independence. This is a slow and halting process, overcoming decades of dependency, and interspersed with pauses for desperate clinging. Freedom one moment and almost despair the next. Sometimes the most difficult treasures for the expiring to release are foolish things like tennis rackets or an old fishing hat.

The task of totally letting go may be too much if we wait until death looms near. We begin to die well the first day we learn to cherish the world we know without crippling dependency on it. Many of the undiagnosed diseases in our daily lives will contribute to anguish near death unless a cure is found. Greed for material goods and leaning too heavily on those we love are diseases that decimate peace near death.

Patients denied permission to die will necessarily expire in a cruel isolation, struggling alone with burdens better shared. Rarely will they have their chance to let go of life if friends will not let go of them. Patients who cannot or will not release their hold on life's treasures, insisting upon hoarding to the end, will die in disappointment and near despair. Resentment and hostility will haunt them. Jealousy will gnaw at any peace. They deny themselves any outlet for the guilt and fearful impotence inside.

Throughout human history, recorders of deathbed scenes tell of a frequent and strange phenomenon. They note that the visage of the newly deceased is quite often wreathed in a gentle smile or in a look of uncommon peace. Interpreters offer many explanations, all of them guesses. Hagiographers report their saints and martyrs have seen their God. Non-believers claim that nature has her own mechanism for euphoria, an analgesic when all systems cease. My guess is that the smile or look of peace reflects a satisfaction limited to men of any creed who died in peace. They expired without earthly strings of any kind choking their hearts and they realized that they had bequeathed no strings to choke the hearts of those they left behind.

In a little less than three months, Gabe was dead. There was a gentle smile on his face when Helen found him. Father Kinton and Dr. Trapp joined Helen in regular and confronting visits of reparation, as long as Gabe was conscious. Then only Helen came until the end.

# 5.
# An Experiment: A Therapy Group for Grievers

A week ago, Maria mysteriously disappeared one afternoon and evening to have a legal abortion against her husband's wishes. Three children, she said, were enough. Maria had always been a love to everyone. Now she is a crab to anyone within reach. Maria seems regularly depressed, unsmiling, curt and sullen in her universal standoffishness.

Nobody seems to understand that Maria is in mourning, grieving the loss of her wanted but unwanted child. Only that segment of her that longs for job promotion and upward mobility endorsed the operation. The remainder felt the echo of family and church admonitions that abortion was tantamount to murder.

Maria remembers well her Mexican traditions of publicly mourning when someone's life ends. After losing her baby, she feels the full force of human grief, but cannot discover a socially acceptable way to express it. So she lives out her sadness and hidden tears in the best way her adopted culture allows: keeping busily productive. She feels compelled to swallow her grief.

Deposits of unfinished grief reside in more American hearts than I ever realized. Until these pockets are opened and their contents aired openly, they block unimagined amounts of human growth and potential. They can give rise to bizarre and unexplainable behavior while causing untold internal stress. When someone dear dies a normal death, the bereaved acquire societal permission to mourn a while and openly, though increasingly the bereaved confess their perplexity over mourning customs and how long grieving should last. They tell of a terrible guilt when their expressions of grief seem insufficient or too prolonged. Nobody offers a norm, yet all of us watch each other, sometimes critically. Grieving consciences are confused and, like Maria, many Americans prefer acting out their grief to risking criticism.

The existence of grief and the need to mourn are seldom identified when we undergo violent loss or separation short of death. Little children who feel rejected in their family circle will sometimes grieve inconsolably for years, acting out their loss of love in complex patterns of behavior. Sudden and unwanted divorces, military separations, imprisonment and placement of children in foster homes, are only samples of situations that cause grief as painful as that following a death. Sudden changes in location can cause young and old to mourn when close friends or relatives are left behind without much promise for future contact.

Homesickness is a form of grieving and responds to the same treatment in psychological therapy. Immigrants grieve in their new land, children at summer camp, students in dormitories and unwed mothers grieve for babies released by adoption. Lost jobs and lost pets, lost dreams and lost reputations, are all samples of countless upsetting situations that warrant our better understanding of human grief.

What is the human feeling of grief? It is an abiding and pervasive sense of sadness over being separated from a person, place or object important to our emotional life. And we refer to mourning as the manifold expressions of this grief. This describes grief in the idyllic sense, but in reality, it is far more complex. Human grief can be as vast and as distinctive as the relationship that is severed.

Listening to mourners in an accepting atmosphere where they dare expose the full range of their loss-shattered feelings confirms how much besides love binds human friends and families together. So, far more is involved in grief than the simple sadness consequent on the loss of love. Our ties to persons bring prestige and sexual thrills, security and fear, freedom and imprisonment, joy and hate, greed and gaiety, indeed, the entire spectrum of human rewards and punishments. Loss or separation will stimulate individual reactions in a unique way. Nobody's grief will ever be like mine. My loss of dentures can be more painful for me than your loss of a friend to you. Animal lovers sometimes grieve the death of a poodle with more intensity than a brother's death in war. There are similarities in our feelings and reactions, but human grief like all human pain is highly personal and distinctive.

Our national customs tend to squeeze all mourners into an identical caricature. We expect and encourage no more than displays of sadness and tears, that stylized demeanor of widowhood, as traditional and public responses to the loss of someone near. We have no customs, no folk expressions, no sympathy cards, hardly any concepts, that allow a comforter to express sympathy in a manner that fits the uniqueness of a friend's grief. Nearly identical words of condolence are forwarded to those bereaved by tragic or sudden death as to those bereaved by lingering illness. And their comfort needs differ so vastly. Survivors are categorized and treated almost the same whether they lost an ancient father or a promising youngster. The tearless widow is a brave heroine or an ungrateful hussy, while the tearful widow is usually considered more loving. It is considered inappropriate to openly vent emotions other than sadness. We compel one another to appear sad when death strikes, even when we know sadness does not always accompany personal loss and that sadness rarely rides alone.

The results can be inhumane and even cruel. The need of sympathizers to succeed in their role as comforters often determines how the bereaved dare express their grief. Yesterday, my brother told of returning from the crematorium stopping for a few beers with a relieved and almost happy widower, only to find the widower's partner on the front porch, all dressed in black, obviously anxious to do his duty of tearful comforting. Mourners find it rarely possible to take the lid off the cauldron of their mixed emotions. Instead of assisting, we can unwittingly add new pain to an already heavy heart, causing the common reaction: "I ought not feel the way I do!"

Until recently, most of my experience with human grief was on a one-to-one basis. Usually I offered sympathy from the religious posture of a clergyman. People seemed to expect spiritual comfort, or I expected them to expect it. I explained every death in terms that would justify the survivor's continued belief in God and church. Around my Roman collar there was no room for irreligious attitudes or superstition. Rare slips of blasphemy or any profanity were followed by a quick comma and an apology. I heard no sighs of relief, no picayune haggling over wills, no testimony of resentment for the dead. All grief arose in the atmosphere of sadness and holiness I carried with me. Mary, Christ's mother, was the model for any widow, St. Augustine for widowers.

Lately, I tried bringing grievers together in therapeutic groups to deal with their unfinished task. Some of the dynamics and results amazed me. I learned more about human grief in a few groups than ever before. No longer did I provide spiritual iodine to daub on surface scratches. I came as fellow griever, a friend who had lost a vocation to which he was totally dedicated for fifteen years, as a searcher who had more questions than solutions. All feelings and attitudes were legitimate. No "oughts" or "shoulds" to impose in limiting each other's feelings. Our motto in coming together was simple: Feel what you feel and trust enough to dare share your feelings with others.

The group experience I will describe began after a public announcement in a class on thanatology. To insure the anonymity of group members, all names and identifying details were changed. No fees were charged the seven women and one man who responded. I invited a kindly mortician to co-facilitate, hoping his experience with groups of mourners might supplement my lack. And I admit to a curiosity about how morticians handled the process of grief. An arbitrary limit of five sessions was imposed before beginning. If more sessions were needed, we would reassess after five.

Our first session consisted mainly in getting acquainted by sharing the loss that brought us together as unfinished grievers.

• Polly, an elegant and polished widow in her late forties, hosted the group and did the planning. Several months before on the sixteenth tee of the country club, when she turned from washing her ball, she had found her husband dead, the victim of a heart attack. His open heart surgery four years before hinted an early death and prompted early retirement, allowing an unusual amount of time together. Polly claimed to still be in shock, forever wondering if her deferred grief might come rushing forth at any moment. Dick's clothes remained in the closets, his belongings on the desk and in the drawers. Life with two sons proceeded for Polly as if he might return at any time. His pipe was on the table.

• Coleen, once divorced and darkly attractive in her late twenties, lost her mother by suicide almost a year before. Dreams consistently took Coleen to an imaginary deathbed where her mother died in ever-changing ways, some serene and some traumatic, none of them suicidal. Coleen was fulfilling her wishes in her dreams, willing to accept any nonsuicidal demise. In our group sessions she dealt effectively with "ordinary" death in her own family and with suicide in others', but not with self-destruction by one of her own. At each mention of her mother's suicide, tears glistened in her dark eyes. She obviously resented her mother for making a daughter so ashamed. She kept demanding her mother to come back and die again, this time in a more acceptable fashion.

• Terrie had lost her fiancé in the Vietnam war six months before. She is a schoolteacher. In her sexually sultry voice, she told of waiting until age twenty-eight for marriage, refusing numerous suitors, finally settling on Todd, a West Point graduate. Todd was expected home momentarily for marriage when word preceded him that he had earned the Congressional Medal of Honor and lost his life defending his men. Her measured tones discounted his heroism as foolhardiness. Since his military burial, Terrie failed at every effort to rebuild her own life. The reason grew clear as she piled halo after halo on Todd's dead head. No living man could measure up to her recollections and Todd's resurrection seemed imminent.

● Cassandra, a motherly and soft-spoken brunette of forty-four, caused a gasp around the room as she told of mothering ten children. Caught in the Catholic dilemma, Cassie looked neither old nor tired enough to do what she had done—Cindy, her second youngest, entered the world with a clubfoot and a lingering heart murmur. While undergoing routine heart surgery at age seven, Cindy suddenly died. Cassie had been unable to release her true feelings to anyone she knew. Religious comfort helped none at all. All her feelings were denied, buried behind a compulsive return to college and the escape of nighttime nursing in a convalescent home where she often pondered: "Why Cindy instead of one of these?"

Cassie was exasperated at hearing and rehearing that she should not miss Cindy with so many other living children at home. Nobody understood, she said, how love and guilt intensified at each new opening of her womb. While struggling to make each new arrival loved and special, she found less and less time for the others. She had had too little time for Cindy alive, and now spent far too much time in resentment. Cassie needed redemption as a mother.

● Julie captured honors for the saddest story in our opening round, largely because of her tearful way of telling it. Four happy years of marriage had terminated eighteen miserable years in her own and foster homes. Her mother and father divorced and in the settlement both disowned nine children. Julie told of awaking one night to find her dearly beloved twenty-eight-year-old husband choking in a chair. He was gone before she could summon anyone, dying in Julie's arms, nestling next to his first child in Julie's womb.

Now with a fourteen-month-old daughter, Julie wanted to find a happiness she had never known without her husband. Few friends stood by her now, impatient with her easy and incessant tears. Julie appeared reluctant to shed her new way of relating to people, no longer an orphan, now the widowed mother of one. At any time, in any place, she could be expected to play the role.

• Macey, a mid-thirtyish widow, had buried her husband less than a month before. Her major concern was over the appropriate length of her mourning. Relatives, friends and fellow church members frowned on her dating or travel, constantly dropping in to share tears or send her little clippings for widows. Twice the owners of adjacent cemetery lots called to complain about the shabbiness of her plot, and, by innuendo, of her love. Macey related how her widowhood actually began when her husband's cancer was diagnosed as fatal; she then mourned to satiety through two years of horrible dying. Six times she took him to the hospital for the final agony and five times she brought him home to barely live some more. She shared with us her relief in coming home alone the sixth time, a relief she is unable to show judging friends who will not rest until grief cripples her again as it did when her husband became addicted to morphine and had a prefrontal lobotomy. Her friends want to see her dressed in funereal black when her needs are for frilly feminine things. Macey sheepishly confessed how she sneaked out to bars unescorted, far from home, feeling guilty about going but at the same time thrilled at being able to dance again, to be held close, to relate to a man as woman instead of as nurse or widow.

• Olivia was a portly woman in her late thirties whose parents had died three weeks apart. An only child, Olivia found in their deaths permission for her to explore a new freedom denied by their lifelong intrusions into her personal and emotional affairs. First she experimented with the extra-marital dating game until her husband caught her and threw her out of the house. She moved down the block into her parents' home, leaving her three teenage boys to fend for themselves and their dad.

It is almost a year since her tragedies but nothing in her parental home has changed. It is like a mausoleum. Kept just as they were at their death, her parents' clothes, dishes, knickknacks, heirlooms, family albums and truck, all speak hauntingly to her, sandpapering her guilt. Meanwhile, Olivia grows fatter, now far too plump to cause much stir in the second marriage market. Her husband refuses to file for divorce, preferring to vent his rage by painting and land-scaping the house, spitefully carrying out the very plans to which she had looked forward the most.

Olivia cannot face either reconciliation or divorce. The price of reunion would be the loss of her promising freedom or another rejection. Yet she also realizes, perhaps uncon-sciously, that divorce would all too soon cost her the illusions she cherishes about finding an attractive husband once she is free to lead the swinging life. Enjoyment of any kind eludes her, fretful over her boys, worried about her husband, sensing the peering and the pointing from neighbors, confronting her ballooning, guilt-ridden image in her dead mother's mirrors. So she works and drinks and sometimes dates in the emp-tiness of her grief-laced conflicts.

• Van did not appear to belong in our grieving group at first. A handsome corpsman in the navy, intense and terror-eyed, Van told of his perennial need to anticipate his parent's death. He was obsessed with their imagined death and his equally imagined grief. Nightly, he pictured them in caskets, waked and buried them, unable to sleep until he prefelt his untested grief.

Van became increasingly edgy at each tale of sorrow and volunteered to leave since his tale could not compare. Julie lashed out at him as some kind of creep or Peeping Tom who got extra jollies by listening to the actual grief of others. Coleen indicted him as a possible pervert. When anger subsided, all concurred in his membership. The consensus was that his problems might lend perspective not to mention that Van was the only male participant.

Near the end of our first session, my co-leader Tony told the group that his true vocation was funeral director. We thought it best to hide his occupation until all could know him as a person. "He doesn't seem like an undertaker!" was the unanimous endorsement for his staying. His introduction prompted several horror stories about funeral directors, and most members expressed a wish to have known Tony when their own shocking experience had happened.

With this cast of characters our group was underway. Our mutual hope lay in a simple objective: to discover if the grieving could somehow better understand and offer superior assistance to one another.

Our first session confirmed that "there is no grief like *my* grief." Cassie, the mother of ten, was first to tell her story. All listened carefully as Cassie cited how the dying little Cindy had grown daily more loving and loved, a sickly queen of the entire household. Family life had come to center around her, and her death sent panic through everyone. Cassie could not admit to the slightest relief at being free of her daily burden of six years, the constant nursing, the denying of everyone else's needs to pay the ever mounting medical bills. All she could share was her deep resentment and guilt. "Was this my punishment from Our Lord for not wanting more children and for practicing contraception?"

The room was heavy in silence. Members grew misty-eyed, then openly tearful. It soon became evident that few tears were for Cassie and her Cindy. Most were reserved for self and personal memories. Suddenly I knew when a grieving group could rightfully terminate, and this insight proved later to be true. Extended or unfinished grief begin to be over when a mourner can rise above personal anguish and reach out to another in comfort.

We learned another facet of this same lesson in our inaugural session. Group members felt the burden of their personal grief by comparing the magnitude of their own loss to the seemingly lesser losses of all others. "But you had children as memories of your love, imagine being without a living memory!" "You had your love for twenty-five years, I had mine for less than one!" "Can you imagine how hard it is to overcome thirty years of closeness? You hardly know each other in the first five or ten years!" Each tale was told as if to top all other tellers. Comparisons galore, overtones of bragging, each voice unwilling to be still until all hearers would concede: "There is no sorrow as great as yours!" And to one who understands the individuality of grief, each grieving voice speaks a truth.

In our second session, Cassie again became first focus. Her musings wandered aimlessly through the death and burial of her dead daughter, the general awfulness of it all for a family of ten, the absence of comfort of any kind. Tears came mechanically as she retold her sufferings to anyone patient enough to continue listening. Finally and gently I confronted her. "Cassie, have you ever really given Cindy your permission to die?"

"I never did and I don't believe I ever could!" Cindy's death had obviously deprived Cassie of her essential image as a loving and worthwhile mother. Slowly, Cassie came to understand. Nonmechanical tears accompanied her admission of an abiding resentment of her sickly daughter, the attention she demanded and received, the time she took, the money spent, and all she left to Cassie were guilt and frustration in motherhood. Cassie was indirectly demanding Cindy's return until she could perfect her damaged image as a worthwhile mother.

Cassie was clearly an effective mother and an attentive wife. Goodness and concern oozed from all of her. Yet, she could not or would not face her little daughter's image and say with all her heart: "It's okay for you to die, Cindy dear!" Cassie needed to control her world and was frozen in rage and resentment when she could not.

It took time and gentle support from the entire group to initiate the thaw. The group members came physically closer and several helped Cassie put the image of Cindy on her lap. She held and fondled her shild, staring at the misshapen foot and looking lovingly into her eyes, saying over and over again without any reservation: "I understand, Cindy. It was all right for you to die. I give you my permission and mother loves you very much."

While Cassie rocked and talked softly to her re-created Cindy, Terrie left the room. Coleen began to sob quietly as she shared her own repeated efforts at giving her mother permission to expire. At first no mention was made of suicide. Coleen needed to grant two permissions, one for death, a second for dying in "such an unacceptable way." As an affront, death was almost manageable for Coleen. Suicide was not. Slowly, as she shared her recent dreams, she understood how each dream regularly re-created her mother's death into a less disgraceful style.

Never have I experienced more raw and exposed emotion in a therapy group than when Coleen put her mother in a nearby chair and began to dialogue over Cassie's sobbing. Coleen denied her mother's right to take her own life and insisted she could never say "yes" to suicide. As she continued, Coleen found her "could not" was a "would not," a bull-headed choice, and she visibly softened. "How could you do this to me, Mother? You were my best friend besides being my only mother. I brought you all my troubles and you said you brought yours to me. Then you disgraced me before my friends, making everyone believe you had no one to talk with, and all the while I was waiting . . ."

Finally, and with sobs of relief, Coleen told her mother it was all right to die the way she chose. "To hell with my friends, Mom! You are my mother and my best friend and I can accept you any way you are!" Coleen had found the beginning to the end of her unfinished grief and looked tired but ecstatic.

While Coleen was chatting with her mentally resurrected mother, Terrie returned composed and anxious to deal with her own unwillingness to allow the death of her fiancé. The group was exhausted and when all insisted upon helping Terrie, I began to believe that maybe grievers were unusually adept at aiding peers. Terrie's voice lost its beauty and measured tones as she told acidly of her loss, again inflating Todd's image beyond credibility. She was not ready to have her illusion burst too quickly. Too much hung in the balance. It explained her social withdrawal, her personal ineffectiveness and her refusal to date any of the eligible men her mother kept suggesting.

Treading lightly I hinted that it took a beautiful and deeply sensitive person to recognize such surpassing beauty as she found in Todd. It worked. Terrie slowly realized how she was projecting her fondest wishes onto Todd's dead image. Now she candidly told of fights and bickering, how they broke up numerous times, as she began to experience the unfinished quality of her grief in the love-hate relationship that bound her to Todd.

Terrie found much of her grief locked in her own stubborn refusal to let Todd be what he wanted, a military man, an heroic officer, a truly fine but very human being. She understood how only Todd would ever know the bravery or foolhardiness in his heroism. She was using her version of what she considered his "wasted life in that goddamn war" as reason and excuse for wasting her own best years. No man, no friend, not even the children she taught, were allowed to know any more than the artificial composure that hid the bitterness in her unfinished grief.

Group members were game to help Terrie bring Todd into the room for a final farewell. The reality in Terrie's role-playing was underscored when she began by fighting with Todd. Slowly she displayed what the observant already knew: her relationship was far from idyllic. She apologized for days without contact, for pettiness in not writing, for dates where not a word was spoken, for using her sexuality as his reward for being good. When Terrie finally said "okay" to his upsetting of her plans, a freshet of kindness appeared in her. Her unfinished grief was finishing.

Terrie's problems went beyond Todd. Her role-playing highlighted her involvement in a who-could-grieve-the-most competition with her own long-since widowed mother. Bereaved when Terrie and her brother were in teens, her mother had struggled to raise her family. Behind Terrie's frustrated personal efforts to live without Todd she repeatedly heard the echo of her mother's protestations of undying love for Dad. To begin a new life, of course, would mean Terrie had lost the battle with her mother for the family grieving championship. Any admission of a new lover, by the same token, meant that her mother had loved more lastingly. And each attempt at fun meant having to listen to her mother's unspoken plaint: "Not yet! Look at me, all these years of going it alone!" Mother suggested many new men, but Terrie secretly wanted the crown as champion.

Terrie learned she also needed to bring her mother into focus and say, "Okay, Mom, you win!" In the ensuing weeks, as Terrie backed out of competition, her interminable grief was lifting. It would take time to cease completely, but Terrie now knew another and better path back to living.

In the third session, Polly taught us much about deferred grief and the refusal to mourn. Her lesson began when I risked confronting her with my honest feelings. She appeared to be going through the motions of being the classic widow, the Jacqueline Kennedy of the Seventies. She kept all of us at a respectful distance with her elegant manners and her dignified role-playing. She blanched when others told her they felt left outside the scope of her honest feelings and true concern. It seemed as if her contributions to the group were broadcast by loudspeaker for the whole world to hear, directed to no one in particular. I said I felt like anyone-at-all in her presence and instead wanted to be someone special, me.

"I promoted and organized this group," she responded sharply. "I invited you all to my home, and I resent . . ." Polly's beginning anger felt better than her polite aloofness. Gentle prodding and group support enabled her to admit she kept herself purposely in a state of suspension, resolute against the pain of grief and the indignity of grovelling in tears. She acknowledged that her tendency to act strong and independent was no more than deep fear of her dependency. Never again would Polly allow herself to feel the full anguish of loneliness and hurt still so vivid in a host of bygone losses.

Polly chose to live out the denial of her innermost feelings and to bask in the admiration of friends who mistook her total refusal to mourn for a quick recovery. She had disallowed the fact of her husband's death from her conscious self, finding surface composure in a round of continuous golf, bridge, parties and travel, forever haunting the places she had formerly gone with her husband, now using her willing but unsuspecting sons as surrogate husbands. To Polly, mourning openly meant rekindling pain she had foresworn. It meant the loss of dignity and control. And Polly was not quite ready.

Anyone reaching out to Polly was treated with routine and proper kindness, becoming a generalized human being, a citizen of the world instead of a distinctive friend. Now she could admit this chilling distance did not begin at widowhood. It originated in youthful tragedies and rejections, in moving away from close family and friends, and it grew in a temporary marital separation, in deaths of close friends, climaxing in the risky open-heart surgery her husband had undergone. Experience had schooled Polly to know grief was more than she wanted to bear. So she stood a step away from any human closeness that would cause such dreadful hurt if it were taken away.

Finally it came. Polly enacted for us the scene on the golf course when she turned to see her fallen husband. Before feeling his pulse or stooping to hug his ebbing warmth, she demonstrated how she stared and screamed: "Goddamn you!" In that scream she clammed up more tightly than ever before, refusing to let death or any violent separation ever again jangle her battered emotions. She climbed above the pain into a pose that could prevent most hurt. She refused intimacy with anyone ever again. In that refusal was caged the deferral of her grief.

Polly began to cry. Mere moistness at first, then full and hearty tears. Maybe her dignity was gone for others to admire, but her warmth for loving became obvious. The group could be felt reaching out in readiness for an explosion that did not come. Polly had only begun to learn how to break out of that timeless suspension in which she was vegetating. She chose to begin her grief in private, and the group respected her choice, knowing it was not another deferral because of the new warmth we all felt in her presence.

Deferral of grief and the refusal to mourn are common today. The dry-eyed widow or widower is not usually as calloused and unfeeling as the public sometimes assumes. Maybe they have already finished their grief, as Macey said she had. Some few may be emotionally upset enough to warrant psychiatric assistance. More often I think we will find the tearless bereaved to be sensitive persons who were frequently hurt in life, their feelings bruised badly by repeated losses or vexing separations. A death in the immediate family, a parental divorce or maybe several, new homes and new schools, bankruptcy or the death of a favorite horse, any one of such losses, any combination of them, could be responsible for closure of the self. Or it could be a distinctive, even mysterious loss, that nobody else could fathom, one too painful to relive or to relate.

Whatever the specific cause for refusing to mourn openly, the individual had simply experienced too much pain before. The floodgates of grief remain locked against any repetition. In counseling college students daily, I often find the mourning record of students has already become quite overwhelming at an early age. Every feeling of closeness or desire for commitment remains harbored carefully inside. Only surface relationships and temporary alliances are allowed. Never again will they love with reckless passion or depend on someone or something with similar fixation. The hurt is too piercing when the bond is broken. Only considerate and patient friends can help unleash past grief by coaxing them into new closeness. And when friends fail, professional help is needed.

Our third session provided some unimagined aspects of anticipatory grief. Van wasted countless hours each night in trying to predict his feelings when his parents would die. Van's parents were still blessings to medicare, healthy, alert and mobile. But he told eerie tales of praying by their bier, standing before their open grave and visiting the cemetery, always testing his feelings in advance.

Van cited numerous disappointments in life, his failure in college, his disloyal fiancé, his violent separation from buddies in Vietnam. While his naval career whisked him around the world, his mother and father remained the center of his identity. Every ounce of grief he could feel was spent ahead of time, as if he could finish mourning at his own pace instead of when death demanded.

Van began to grasp glimmers of truth about himself. His endless and futile attempts at anticipatory grief were ineffective masks for his own personal fears of death which he could not release. Van required the right of kingship over every deeply emotional situation in life. He attended courses on thanatology, attended our grieving group and volunteered for extra duty in the intensive care units, all the while fantasizing about other persons' deaths, as a kind of protection against facing his own. All talk of matters moribund were kept at surface level, helping Van save face in pretending to confront what he most deeply feared: his own personal passing. Van learned how he had already begun the mourning process for Van, while displacing his grief onto the fancied deaths of those he could legitimately grieve for.

Macey taught us about a more common and more effective brand of anticipatory grief. Friends failed to grasp that her grief had ended long before her husband died. She needed their endorsement to launch a new life now instead of waiting until friends and relatives caught up with her. She told of missing her husband long before he died, letting him go dozens of times, sometimes for practice, just in case. She had participated haltingly in all hopeful talk of cures, of a trip to Lourdes, of a quack in Mexico, fantasizing all the while about new husbands, a new career, a new home, romance and excitement, her imagination fired by the favorite possibilities that gave her the strength to stand by a ravaged husband through two years of ugly dying. Fantasy made it purgatory instead of hell.

Macey asked little more than the group's blessing on the new life of her dreams. She wanted support in rebuilding instead of remaining glued to memories of drug addiction, cancer smells, unpayable bills and unpredictable doctors. She wanted her youngsters to know healthy men almost as much as she wanted it for herself. In the group she found endorsement for taking a Tahiti trip for singles. No more sneaking to bars, now she could walk in the front door hand-in-hand with men who called. She worried still about losing friends who would not correct their caricature of widowhood. She began to know they would return as friends when they saw her happiness, or they were not friends at all.

In our fourth session, Julie exhibited the terrors of excessive mourning and how it can border on emotional illness. Julie was now in mourning for upwards of fifteen months. An overtone of bragging marked each retelling of her plight as forgotten widow. "Nobody ever had a childhood as screwed up as mine. I cry because my perfect marriage and all happiness were taken away. Nobody can possibly replace him. I wish I knew somebody who would adopt the baby and I would commit suicide." This was the message underlying the bulk of Julie's talk. A new lilt of pride in her voice, a new swagger in her tones, as she continuously came on as the longest-suffering widow in the West. Her tears and saddened face were tools to keep everyone away so she could bask in the emotional rewards of martyrdom.

No considerate and sensitive mortal will tell another how long or how hard to mourn. But when mourning becomes a way of life, a new style for relating to everyone and for gaining inordinate attention, I believe it at least borders on the excessive. When mourning is clearly a defense against any new beginning and offends or harms those who love us, violating or preventing present love in supposed testimony to love past, then it has grown excessive. Widowhood can be a convenient cocoon for protection against the normal responsibilities and vicissitudes of life. And for Julie it was.

The group ganged up on Julie, pushing her ever less gently into full realization of what her grief was doing, of how incredible it had become. She began to see that even saints grow tired of too many tears and even best friends cannot stand a constant dose of self-pity and bragging at each meeting. The dying grow tired of talking about death, the living even more so. Julie impishly began to admit that her shield of widowhood reflected intense fear of sex and dating, her overall fear of males, and especially her fear of being unable to find a man who could accept the poor image she had of herself.

Underlying excessive grief is usually a conviction of having failed the deceased. Cassie feels it in overmourning Cindy and Julie feels it in her never-ending grief. At last Julie can share how she indulged in fits of petulance and violent temper. She understands how the confusion in her past was vented in her marital relationship, in sexual coldness, in pettiness and insane jealousy. Her false mourning shouts the tarnished beauty of a love that could have sparkled if she had been more loving. She fears ever trying again. It is simpler to boast of a loss than to risk another failure.

Julie is not unusual. Mothers who failed or spoiled their offspring grasp for new stature as mothers of supereminent love by the length and depth of their sorrow. Widowers reveal that their prolonged grief is no more than self-punishment for treating a wife coldly. And all of us know the intricate examining we do when death strikes close. It is tempting to mourn louder and longer than sorrow warrants when the conscience hurts for not having loved more or better.

Our fourth session began with rejoicing over the encouraging changes we noted in each other. Coleen told about her dream of a massive funeral where she talked openly of her mother's suicide at a post-funeral feast. She stood receiving condolences without a whimper in apology or defense. On three nights she dreamed of life instead of the usual death.

Terrie told of having fun on a date her mother arranged and how she jokingly crowned her mother queen of the family grievers.

Julie's progress caused as much hilarity as her original tale had sadness. She reported her first date for dinner and dancing, and she was still languishing over the kiss she received, ". . . right on the lips, too."

Polly exuded new warmth, hugging members on the way in and out, determined to lower all barriers to beginning intimacy. She tittered in telling how she refused her golf pro's invitation for dinner and how she regretted it since. She now cried in bed and had sent the first load of her husband's belongings to the Salvation Army. She had freed her sons from their escort role and noticed how her tears gave them freedom to shed their own.

Cassie had made least progress. While winning her battle over Cindy's death, news came that her dad was dying. Her fear of releasing all hold on Cindy was intensified by her anticipatory fear of saying goodbye to her father. And Cassie did not feel any more worth as daughter than as mother.

Joy was everywhere when we noticed Olivia was day-dreaming—a hundred miles away. Polly reached out to her and Olivia told quietly of her inability to deal with the love and hate relationship she felt toward her parents and saw being acted out in her own life. Her carousing and avoidance of family responsibility terminated in lonely nights, with every momento of her folks seeming to join the neighborhood's staring eyes and wagging tongues in deepening her guilt for abandoning her home.

Everyone listened. Some members encouraged an immediate return home, others encouraged a full dose of the swinging life to avoid future regrets. The courage Olivia needed to deal with her husband came from the unanimous suggestion to try a talk. The day was drawing near when she could confront her husband, risking her new freedom and a possible rejection, in working on a marriage long retarded by her own unwillingness to grow old without an adolescence.

Tony, the funeral director, never became personally involved. My suspicions were confirmed. He knew no more than most about the grieving process and how to minister effectively. Insightful quotes and memorized gems of folk wisdom were as close as he dared come. His noninvolvement in the grief of customers is not caused by their number as much as by the failure of his school of mortuary science to teach him any more than embalming skills and business techniques. His presence taught all of us that modern mourners need more than the help of kindly but untrained undertakers if they are to find emotional and personal growth through mourning.

Our fifth session was mostly for Olivia and for deepening lessons others had learned. At the end I believed we needed no more sessions. Everyone was far from the finish line, but all were on the right path to therapeutic mourning. The group provided each member with new freedom to make a choice of beginning anew or of resorting to the painful but sometimes useful paralysis of unfinished grief.

Are grievers more effective in helping other grievers than nongrievers would be? I am not yet sure. We will try again and again. Now I only know that with peers, grievers find instant honesty, much cross-understanding, much reflection of self in others, all resorting in a short-cut through so much of what ordinarily keeps unfinished grievers from letting go.

I did learn that we need more than current wakes and funerals to help the grieving reestablish their lives among the living. Maybe when funeral directors lose increasing business in embalming, caskets and earth burial, they will begin to recoup their losses by sponsoring groups where their patrons can grieve together. Until then, it will help each of us to better understand the dynamics of human grief. These I hope to clarify in the next chapter.

# 6.
# Understanding
# Human Grief

I was nervous all day. Early that morning the pastor assigned my first solo wake as a priest for eight o'clock the same evening. All day I rehearsed my words of comfort for the widow. Before the bathroom mirror, I practiced ways of looking proper and walking correctly. At every break in a complicated day, I reflected on my major concern: when and how to leave gracefully.

The only part in my assignment I knew well was how to say the rosary. Even there I checked the five sorrowful mysteries. My mind kept sorting dozens of "dos" and "don'ts" catalogued from altar boy days. Theoretical ideas from seminary training rose to the fore, anxious for a test.

I arrived at the funeral home fifteen minutes early. I missed the parking spot reserved for the clergy, happy to park in the shadows for one final and unseen rehearsal. The deceased was a thirty-five-year-old father of four who had died unexpectedly. He was a Protestant, but since he attended Mass each Sunday, the pastor and his widow agreed a rosary would be fitting. Pastoral orders made me mindful of all the non-Catholics who would be present, fair game for my good example, prospective converts. My plan was simple: calmness, appearance of near normalcy, allowing widow and family to react at their own pace without my affording any cues. The only book I had found recommended this.

Once inside, traces of spookiness came over me, the instant and eerie quiet, the sedate and formal manners of the undertaker as he took my hat and coat. Without a look or a word, shoulders high and head cast slightly down, I moved through a growing crowd toward the open casket. Ignoring the family for a moment, I knelt for a customary private prayer, apparently staring into the dead man's face. Actually I was lost in another final rehearsal.

I rose solemnly and blessed myself slowly, walking directly to where the widow sat surrounded by her children and family. I smiled at the children, recognizing them from the schoolyard, and stooped toward their mother. "Hello, Mrs. Prague, I am Father Kavanaugh. How are you?"

Nothing in my repertoire could possibly have prepared me for her response. "How in the hell do you think I am! That's my husband there in the casket and these are my fatherless children, and . . ."

A gentle hand reached out to quiet her. It was not mine. I wish now it had been, but I could barely breathe. In a moment she held out her hand for mine, looking up only long enough to say: "I'm sorry, Father."

All emotional systems inside me roared. While I appreciated the soothing and mechanical comfort of the rosary, my mind was left free to rehearse an exit. Near terror welled up when I approached the family to say goodbye. Afraid to risk a word, I smiled softly, shaking all extended hands and left.

Old Mrs. Cochrane followed me outside. "Father, I've been attending wakes here in our parish for almost twenty years and yours was the finest rosary I ever heard." I should have hugged her and now I would. Then I was too desperate to get outside, to overcome my shame and clear my head. I wanted to try and fathom what occurs in human heads and hearts when grief seems overwhelming. I wanted to get into my car and begin at once a reformation of my style.

What is the proper way to comfort and console a fellow human who has experienced recent grief? My inquiries reveal that few tasks in life cause more anxiety than consoling the bereaved. I have tried dozens of different approaches, ranging from my style with Mrs. Prague to simply being myself. I even tried phony cheerfulness early in life, and in a later period tried endless talking about spiritual interpretations of afterlife. I felt unsure in every posture until I realized that although grief is unique, there are a number of similar phases each grieving person passes through. My point of focus changed from the impression I was making to the griever's needs.

There are seven phases or stages identifiable in the grieving process. Within each of the seven, we can notice typical feelings, distinct reactions to these feelings and definite needs or cries for help. The seven stages we will discuss are shock, disorganization, volatile emotions, guilt, loss and loneliness, relief and reestablishment. The stabilizing force in all human grief is hope, holding the person together in fantasy at first, then in the promise of a new life.

Even this understanding failed to make my consolation sure fire. It did relieve my anxiety to know that the typical feelings and distinctive reactions experienced at each stage in the grieving process are normal and not caused by my clumsiness. At each stage, the grieving react in a rather predictable way, at least within broad guidelines. When permitted free expression, the grieving will reflect their true feelings, exhibit their honest reactions and reveal identifiable needs. I found comfort most effective when my efforts were directed to these special needs which the grieving are only sometimes able to articulate. Touching these needs in a friend is to help him grieve therapeutically.

Upon careful analysis these seven phases in grieving closely parallel the five stages mentioned earlier as observed by Dr. Kubler-Ross in dying patients who are aware of their impending death. The similarity is not artificial or contrived. The dying seem as intent upon mourning their own passing as we are to mourn theirs.

By cataloguing the stages in the grieving process, I hope you will not infer they are in any way separate. Rather, they are distinct emotional states. They invariably intertwine and overlap. Nor are they successive in the order listed or in any order. Shock customarily intones the grieving process, while reestablishment, if reached, means grief is over. In between, the stages vary in almost every conceivable way. Certain stages can be bypassed entirely, while others may last no more than a few minutes. Highly charged feelings like anger are frequently more like flashes than emotional states, and softer emotions like sadness can remain as permanent features in the post-grief personality.

Much like in recovery from heavy drug usage, flashbacks are common in the grieving dynamics. Months or years later, occasionally or repeatedly, certain phases of grief will reoccur with obvious or hidden causes. Birthdays, Christmas and mutual friends are obvious causes, while the less obvious and mysterious causes are hidden still in the complexity that is man in grief.

Only a practiced eye can accurately discern the dominant themes at work and know readily the pressing needs of the griever. Consolation is a human art in which, maybe, only professionals can specialize. But if we fail to gain a beginning understanding of this art, we risk becoming an additional problem for grieving friends. Knowledge of at least the basics can insure that our efforts at consolation will be somewhat therapeutic instead of only well intentioned.

How can you identify a stage of grief? Clues can be readily available to those sensitive enough to watch carefully and to listen permissively. Each stage involves characteristic emotions. And the griever clearly exhibits his needs if we can comprehend the signals. Mrs. Prague was definitely in the phase of disorganization where unusual or uncharacteristic conduct can be expected. If I had pulled up a chair in silence, held her hand and listened for several moments, I could have known her needs, avoiding her embarrassment and mine. Too much preoccupation with how we are coming across can prevent us from noticing obvious cues.

Before inspecting the dynamics of human grief, it helps to understand the effects our personal involvement in the bereavement can have upon the quality of our consolation. When our own heart is grief-stricken, it helps to understand and respect the fact of our own mourning. What stage are we passing through? If uninvolved emotionally, it is easier to be sure that what we observe belongs to the bereaved. When the bereavement touches us, it is easy to displace our own feelings onto others and to reach out to console ourselves in disguise. We end up treating ourselves when we intended to help a friend. How often I have seen this shifting of needs within grieving families. Mother is ashamed of feeling the way she does so she transfers her personal feelings to the children. Dad may put his own feelings on Mom and nobody knows who in the family needs what type of consolation. When our own emotions are upset by the bereavement, honesty and respect for our personal feelings will make us more effective as consolers.

At the announcement that someone dear is dead or terminal, shock is the expected reaction. In this first stage, the real and the unreal worlds crash in collision. The bodily systems gallop while the mind reels in conflict, hearing and rejecting, knowing and blocking, plus a host of individual reactions. Fainting is common, and bizarre conduct is frequent. I remember telling a teenager of his dad's sudden death only to hear him break out into hysterical laughter. Later he apologized for his uncontrollable behavior.

Shortly after the initial shock, disbelief or other forms of denial begin. Everything inside shouts "no" to death. The mind struggles to leave the world or to escape, seeking refuge in the classic but unanswerable "why?" During the period of shock and denial, the best role for any comforter is one of physical presence and permissive listening. Physical touch and a few words of repetitive reassurance are important antidotes.

How tempting it can be for the consoler to ease his own tensions by slipping into the more familiar role of advising, resorting to explanations, religious comfort or clichés from our folk heritage. Time enough later on for any or all of these. Now, mere words cannot be heard. The mind races with ideas and fantasies, often teetering on the brink of a total withdrawal. Emotions rush about unsorted and out of control. To be there is enough. Keeping the griever in touch with a loving part of the world is the primary goal.

Doctors, nurses, military chaplains and police who regularly announce tragic death, need constant reminders that at this point the dying person's mind is not connected for listening. Blocking is its mental salvation. It was listening only moments before and what it heard makes it temporarily unwilling to risk listening again. Even when questions are asked, seldom are answers expected. Questions are more statements of disbelief than actual queries. They are the human way of parrying with reality until control can be restored. Any important information should be deferred until the person in shock is listening again.

When the news of death sinks in, practiced comforters expect an explosion from the more open and outgoing, a sullen and intense withdrawal from the more introverted. Explosions can take the form of hysteria, screaming, pounding or breaking valuable objects. Withdrawal is expressed in a need to run, to cruise in a car, to drink or to lock oneself in a room. Explosions are clearly more therapeutic than withdrawing into oneself, so should be encouraged or at least readily permitted. Explosions lessen the need to escape into a world of make-believe. However, I have found it futile to suppose that introverts will suddenly explode under crisis. And it is cruel to force or encourage what is contrary to their style of emoting.

To step back into the real world from the land of shock and denial is most often a conscious choice. The grieving choose to return when they feel ready. Their return can be expected much sooner if those nearby make the world around them pleasing and warmly accepting, one where they can dare be themselves without being forced to play a distasteful role. The land of shock and denial attract the grieving to a much longer stay when the real world offers no more than the ugliness and chill of death.

The second stage in the dynamics of human grief is one of disorganization. The grieving claim to feel totally out of touch with the ordinary proceedings of life. Their surroundings are out of focus and they draw unwarranted conclusions from flimsy evidence. A friend compared this stage to being stranded in the middle of a fast-flowing stream while water and debris rushed around her, timeless, motionless, helpless. Confusion is the normal reaction to disorganization. Actions can be completely out of character as were Mrs. Prague's. Environment seems alien, names and faces are forgotten, suicide may be threatened, and the griever willingly returns to former periods of life, the more tolerable and happy ones.

The principal need of the disorganized is the consistent physical presence of one they can trust. They need physical contact, hugging or rubbing, caressing or handholding, all designed to assure them of the gentleness and pleasure of a world their mind cannot bring into focus. They need to cry and cry, to talk and talk, without the interruptions of our sanity. The substance of their talk may be foolish, but loquaciousness helps sort it out until they can recapture their thinking powers lost in the myriad of unwanted thoughts and unaccustomed feelings that confuse their mind.

All important decisions about the future or even a funeral should be postponed until disorganization begins to dwindle. If postponement is impossible, all decisions should be made with respect for this crippling state of mind. Wise funeral directors appreciate the confusion in this phase of personality rearrangement, and they know how unscrupulous confreres capitalize on it. I frequently hear my mortician friends object to any deferral of burial, even for two or three days. Yet, if any funeral is to achieve its intended purpose of grief therapy, the bereaved should have moved past their crippling disorganization. Hearts can be permanently saddened by unwise decisions made before the clouds of confusion have lifted.

The third stage, where mourners unleash their volatile emotions, can be the most upsetting to handle. Not many Americans feel comfortable around jealousy, terror, hatred or resentment, especially when they are directed against the newly dead. This stage is in reality several stages combined into one. Each volatile emotion has distinctive features, though there is adequate similarity in a person's underlying needs to warrant discussing them together.

Behind the volatile emotions that the grieving exhibit are the more primary feelings like helplessness, hurt and frustration. These primary feelings are the strains that any effective consolation needs to touch. To hear a gentle friend curse our God or shout invectives at his dead wife is too much for most ears to tolerate. In our eagerness to silence such unsocial and distasteful outbursts, we forget they are but echoes of a still deeper pain within. Friends interrupt these violent monologues with explanations. Doctors tend to tranquilize this phase of grief into groggy acquiescence. Nurses hurry volatile grievers out of hospital wards, partly for hospital peace, partly because few of us feel genuinely at ease within the range of such upsetting demonstrations.

The natural reaction for a mourner caught up in the fury of his own volatile emotions is to deny and bury his feelings out of a sense of shame. "I ought not feel this way! Why do I say such things? Am I losing my mind?" Unless these rebellious feelings are expressed, they simmer harmfully inside, interfering with all possible growth through grieving. Years later we observe mourners still clinging to their anger or rage, their resentment or hate, crushed in the conflict between an open display of their true feelings and their unwillingness to look foolish. Herein lies much of the cause for the physical symptoms like migraine headaches and ulcerative colitis which doctors attribute to unfinished grief. Nobody can estimate the extent of medical bills for treating unexpressed grief.

Not every person wants or needs to vent his volatile

emotions in a similar manner. Some can effectively and therapeutically allow their anger or resentment to surface and simmer away silently in their melancholic sadness. Talking openly and calmly can help the more phlegmatic mourners lose their feelings of rage or jealousy. However, more than a few grieving individuals need violent expressions for their inner turbulence, stifled until they can rant or pound or break.

Whipping posts can play an important therapeutic role. Doctors, nurses, relatives, clergymen or undertakers are valuable therapeutic objects for anger in need of a focus. The self is the least beneficial whipping post and the most difficult for comforters to handle. A wastrel son can handily be blamed for his father's heart attack or maybe a Catholic daughter who married a Jew. Bosses make convenient scapegoats for workers as employees do for bosses. How readily we leap to silence emotional diatribes directed at psychological whipping posts when it might be far more helpful to encourage them. A skilled clergyman told me that if there were no convenient target for the griever's need to blame and lambast someone, he would in good conscience create one.

As a rule, professionals do not make *ideal* consolers. Their contributions are brief and token. Not only does their professional image cast a restrictive pall over emotional freedom, but they need to defend. Doctors and nurses argue defensively for the quality of medical care and hospital treatment. Clergymen often need to justify God's actions and find it hard to allow open anger at a devine scapegoat in their presence. Professionals would instantly improve their effectiveness around grief by knowing that no justification is needed. Mourners are not listening nor are they attacking anyone for real. Their inner hurt and helplessness are bubbling over in a way most satisfying to their personal frustration. An elderly doctor claims to purposely stay away from deathbed scenes, hopefully to draw a therapeutic attack upon himself so that less secure persons might be spared.

Friends who understand the griever's life-style can be the most important antidote when they allow the expression of whatever lurks inside. In permissive listening, the grieving learn their feelings are neither good nor bad, they are merely theirs and there. The greatest mistake I made in my early religious training was to accept the concept that feelings by themselves can be morally bad. In reality, feelings can be no more than neutral. When a mourner receives acceptance and assurance that such violent and unaccustomed feelings are all right, the feelings will gradually run their natural course. Volatile feelings exhaust a person as they are fully felt and ventilated. They have a built-in safety valve that in most cases switches them off long before harmful or foolish actions follow.

One night I listened as a newly bereaved acquaintance screamed threats and invectives for hours against the medical personnel who treated his wife near the end. Everyone in the hospital was either a murderer or an accomplice. All the while he paced past a phone, threatening to summon lawyers and to harass everyone involved, shouting until he was too exhausted to pick up the phone or even to talk above a whisper. The next week his rage had subsided.

The fourth stage grievers pass through is one of guilt. After a meaningful relationship is severed by death, life is relived in panoptic vision, highlighting and magnifying the good that might have been. The saddened want another chance to try, especially a chance to prevent or postpone an untimely death, time to erase any personal neglect or failure. "Maybe I chose the wrong doctor." "If I had only driven her to church . . ." Drinkers regret their drinking, children wish they had visited home more often. Conversations are spiced with "I could have . . ."; "I should have . . ." and "If only . . ." The reality of the past matters little. Even if the deceased died happy, guilt-prone mourners will find abundant reasons to intensify their shame.

Self-deprecation and depression swarm in the wake of guilty feelings. The need to punish oneself prompts the building of impossible plans and promises on top of regrets. "Never again will I . . ." becomes the battle cry of reparation. Open mourning can escalate beyond any true sense of sorrow, designed to prove to self and the outside world that love was deeper than guilt would have us believe. When this new and false mourning is added to deposits of sincere grief, suspicions of personal phoniness compound the guilt in a never-ending circle.

After death, no easy answer is available for guilt of long standing which is based on the mourner's reasonably accurate perception of reality. He may need to make promises of heroic reparations for his failure. At least, he needs to save face by openly vowing to try harder to become the kind of person he now wishes he had been, a walking memorial to a truth only finally learned in death.

Tinkering amateurishly with another's lifelong guilt, offering Kleenex when surgery is indicated, is hardly a proper task for a comforting friend. Only the grief-stricken can properly assess his personal needs to make amends. And until he accepts and begins to perform the penance his conscience assigns, his feelings of guilt will harass him. Patient listening can help open avenues for rebuilding and for finding a second chance to prove himself. All our hollow words and pitying forgiveness will not still his lifelong guilt.

I remember as a priest sitting through the night with a parishioner who had been a lifelong victim of the great thirst.

For thirty-plus years he had promised his newly dead wife that he would stop drinking. His guilt poured out while he now poured bourbon in. His disdainful children would not occupy the same house with him on this night before the funeral, disgusted by his refusal to correct a vice that they claimed had shortened their mother's life. Only a drinking companion and I sat listening to his guilty testimonials. When his comrade was gone and the bourbon, too, he tenderly reached for his wife's picture. Kissing it lovingly, he vowed never to drink again. Lifelong sobriety as a memorial to his wife. I later heard that he stumbled once after the funeral, but never again. Too bad he waited so long. I can only hope that patient and permissive listening helped it happen when it did.

Lesser forms of guilt, like second-guessing a choice of doctors or hospitals, will often dissipate in the telling. More pressing guilts need the acceptance and forgiveness from important people in the mourner's world. The need here is to talk since guilt shared with significant friends will dwindle in a nonjudgmental atmosphere. So many of what sound like cries of guilt are only loud and testing pleas for assurance that there is nothing to feel guilty about. I wish I had a nickel for every word I wasted in trying to explain away the guilt of grieving parishioners. Their need was simply to tell how badly they felt and know they would not be rejected. Instead of listening and allowing them to forgive themselves in my acceptance, I showered them with logic. My guilt for such foolish sincerity is less now that I have shared it.

The sense of loss and loneliness is the fifth stage and many characterize it as the most painful. The full sense of loss never becomes obvious at once. Needs and dependencies in ourselves become gradually apparent, noticing an empty crib, a vacant chair near the TV, an unused pillow, an extra toothbrush, a family photo, a missing letter or phone call. The fullness of loss and the resultant loneliness are often felt long months after consolation is thought necessary.

Even in what outsiders characterize as miserable relationships, where only pseudo-tigers growled and fought, the sense of loss can be as acute as in relationships that seemed idyllic. Fighting and bickering join teasing and razzing as ways of showing love that can be fully understood only by those who miss them.

The alcoholic spouse or town ne'er-do-well are missed in ways few can understand unless their own heart is involved. Neighbors are almost relieved enough to send "good riddance" with their reluctant condolences, rejoicing that survivors now have a better chance. And they are puzzled why the family mourns at all for drunks or rousters. If you have never loved and lost a family troublemaker, you may not know the excitement he contributed to family life, the depth of his sober love, the beauty and sincerity in his promises to reform and the full exposure of his humanity for all to jeer or love. This sense of loss and loneliness can be grasped only by the losers, those who always hoped he would have another chance.

As the sense of loss expands, sadness and depression are its natural heirs. Self-pity feeds them both. The heart experiences a vacuum in need of being filled and the search for artificial distractions or quick replacements begins. The lost person grows out of focus in memory, an elf becomes a giant, a sinner becomes a saint, because the grieving heart needs giants and saints to fill an expanding void. Anybody is better than nobody. Being alone adds to the curse of loneliness. Mothers reach out for sons to replace fathers and dads expect daughters to become instant surrogate moms. Friends at a bar can become closer than lifelong friends who are far away.

Quick marriage or remarriage becomes a tempting threat. Adopting another child to replace a deceased one seems unquestionably right. Easy answers all, but any answer will do as long as it soothes the awful pangs of loss.

During those periods when loss is fully felt and loneliness seems unbearable, the frequent and regular presence of a stabilizing friend becomes essential, even if it is only a temporary replacement. Dogs and cats can help, humans can help much more. The ultimate goal in conquering loneliness is to build a new independence or to find a new and equally viable relationship.

Grievers who dearly loved and fully experienced the extent of their loss know that replacement is not possible. What was lost was unique. Only a genuine new love will do to fill the resultant void. The new love can grow in the same ground as the old, share the same life-style and bed, but the roots of any former love are so entwined in the bereaved heart that no new love can uproot or replace them. New loves can only flourish by growing next to former ones, overshadowing and hiding them, perhaps, while somehow making their loss less present and less poignant.

It has been fascinating to hear mourners record the full scope of the void they feel. All the innuendos of that deeply human mystery, of what one human being finds loveable in another, are detected in descriptions of loss. The minute and innumerable threads that bind two human beings together in a relationship, all the interneeds and interdependencies, seem taken for granted until death severs them. Then tiny things like odors and long toe nails, scars and facial wrinkles, the lines of a smile and ways of touching, all become as difficult to forget as bigger treasures like mutual acceptance and sexual fulfillment.

It takes bravery and endurance to allow the depth and

meaning of a lost relationship to be totally experienced. It is tempting to escape in following the American tradition that all pain lessens in keeping busy. Modern life offers many ways of evading the full reach of feeling alone and lonely. A common escape is in a second or third marriage which unfinished grief will strive to restyle into a carbon copy of the love that was lost. It cannot be done. It can be faked and phonied, trying to rediscover the past in the present, all the while preventing new love from blossoming.

How important it is for parents of dead children to finish their grief before trying to recapture in a hapless new child what has been buried. Imagine the identity problems of bearing the name of a brother whose death was the reason for your birth or adoption. Picture how hard it would be to enact the role of a statue representing another child.

If the future is to bring freedom and happiness, it is worth the effort to grieve to completion before seeking a new partner or making any final commitment. The cost can be high in pain and in time, but the ultimate result will be worth all the suffering. I have resolved never to push my grieving friends nor to try to slow them down when they are deciding on a new commitment. I prefer to be their devil's advocate, tempting them to think.

The feelings of relief that characterize the sixth stage are difficult to admit and acknowledge openly. They seem so crude and ungrateful. After a death that has dragged out over many months, even the most intolerant can understand some feelings of relief in survivors. What is difficult, however, is to grasp the normalcy of feeling at least some degree of relief when almost any human relationship is severed, even the most tenderly loving.

Relief after death can come from a number of sources. Obviously, a degree of relief comes when excruciating pain is halted or when medical bills in the thousands of dollars stop soaring. Less obviously, relief also arises when death frees us from the many demands that love can make or when death permits us to sample some of the new relationships our fantasy often promised as more fulfilling and fun than the one we had. Parents tell of feeling relieved of the pressure of being good parents. Husbands and wives tell of relief at not having to measure up to the excessively high standards imposed by a partner, or at not having to produce so zealously for a demanding one.

All brands of human love can be gentle tyrants, mixing the pressures of love's demands with ample rewards. Few, if any, vibrant human relationships when honestly appraised do not coexist with a host of speculations on what it might be like to be free from demands of spouse and children, to taste another style of life, to try another mode of love or sex, to find a still more rewarding answer than present loves seem to offer. In these and similar fantasies reside the causes of the normal relief most mourners feel at the time of death.

Relief at a loved one's death seems so calloused we can barely think about it, let alone discuss it out loud, admitting its presence and its normalcy. Relief is so intermingled with our sense of loss we cannot see it isolated enough to take it for what it is: a normal, human response. The feeling of relief does not imply any criticism for the love we lost. Instead, it is a reflection of our need for ever deeper love, our quest for someone or something always better, our search for the infinite, that best and perfect love religious people name as God. And relief can also be seen as no more than a new expression of our inbred puritan ethic: maybe somewhere else there is a more fulfilling love, and now we are morally freed to seek it.

Unless the normalcy in feelings of relief is admitted, new

shadows of guilt descend. Self-hatred attacks our ingratitude. Shame grows for the apparent rebuke we offer our former love. The grieving at this stage need a confidant capable of relating to this frightening sense of relief without indictment or adding to guilt and shame. They need a loving listener in whose presence they can freely express and tolerate what at first seems to be the most ignoble of human thoughts, relief at a loved one's death.

In time, with help and permission, most grievers can arrive at the final stage of reestablishment. This stage begins slowly for most, hope softening guilt and the sense of loss, fantasies of a new life dotting part of each waking day. As hope and fantasy approach reality, verdant meadows lie ahead, blue skies over open roads, excitement and extended hands—all promises of a new ability to walk alone. Fantasies fade into constructive efforts to reach out and build anew. The phone is always answered, the door as well, and meetings seem important, invitations are treasured and any social gathering becomes an opportunity. Concrete steps replace wild reveries. Mementos of the past are put away for occasional family gatherings. New clothes and new places promise dreams instead of only fears.

Reestablishment never arrives all at once. Anxiety and guilt are too often partners in each beginning effort. The widower feels uneasy in readopting a dating code long since forgotten. He frets at what his family thinks or at how the children would treat a substitute mother. A widow takes a journey to Hawaii, fearful to admit her fun and happiness lest she indict her previous marriage, ashamed to tell her joy, her freedom, her acceptance by new companions. Parents who lost a child join the P.T.A., sponsor a child at camp and adopt an orphan in Indo-China, enjoying their new involvement yet fearful of admitting too soon that their hearts are at ease in new relationships. Guilt engulfs every attempt at reestablishment that might possibly be made too soon. The bereaved have no code of manners and no clear limitations for socially acceptable grief. They want to enjoy while fearing the fun, wondering if they should still be in black or visiting a grave instead of walking toward new life.

Friends are paramount at this stage. Old friends are important for encouragement and permission. New friends can offer realistic opportunities for coming out from under the grieving mantle. With newly acquired friends, the grieving are no longer widows or survivors. They are people. To new friends the entire grieving process seems like an old movie seen too many times already. Life begins at the point of new friendship. All the rest is of yesterday, buried, unimportant to the now and the tomorrow.

Mourners tell of being pushed too fast into a totally new life when they only wanted encouragement. Dates were provided when they only wanted to see a show or visit an old friend, to know it was all right to look and seem happy again. Comforters frequently project their own frustrated needs onto grieving friends, forgetting that reestablishment arrives sooner and lasts longer if opportunities are offered instead of being forced. To launch out into a new life before the proper time is only to defer the final launching.

The seven stages of grieving do not subscribe to the logic of the head as much as to the irrational tugs of the heart, the logic of need and permission. The most perplexing problem consolers can face is grasping how much grief has been anticipated. After lengthy dying, only token solace is needed, while much is needed in the months and years that precede. After sudden death, especially if it is untimely in other ways, solace is needed long after most consolers have ceased consoling. With the elderly, the grieving process begins long years before death occurs, spread equally throughout the golden years. Ever since I first caught a glimpse of my dad as an old man, my grief for him began. Now when death comes, I will miss him, but my grief will long since be spent.

To friends who might bring consolation to me when death strikes near, I have one further recommendation. Please bring along your sense of humor. I do not mean your ability to tell funny stories or to make me laugh. I only mean that in your presence I hope to find that sense of perspective that will give focus to my foibles and the foibles in all I love. Grief may well be usually characterized by tears and sorrow, but I hope someone helps me see beyond the sadness to the fun and happiness found in sharing life with another equally as mysterious human being. My own grief will never be finally therapeutic until I have fully revelled in the fact that I loved another and my lost friend in turn loved me.

# 7.
# Children and Death

To coin a title with the words "death" and "children" in it appears to me like the height of incongruity. Children are like definitions of life itself. They seem to bubble over and to foam with vitality. Life seems to be theirs, even the sickly and skinny ones, and death is the property of the old. Children's sparkling eyes and uncomplicated ways shout an innocence and a simplicity I envy. I am temporarily tempted to keep the little ones that way. I think of joining parents and educators who struggle to spare them from any ugliness in our world, especially the ugliness in human death.

This tug toward the protectiveness of children is quite modern. Until less than seventy-five years ago, death and children were more in comradeship. Hardly any large family, rich or poor, did not lose one or more children in the early years of life. My own maternal grandmother could only rear five of nine. My wife's paternal grandmother raised only five of eleven to adulthood. An aura of death and violence hung closer to home. Grandpa would take the older children to a barefisted prizefight, maybe a cock fight or to a hanging. Along city streets brawls or barroom fisticuffs were commonplace. Nearly every child had at least one classmate who died. It was no more unusual to sleep with a dying grandparent than it was near an expiring baby brother.

From interviews with nostalgic oldsters, I surmise that parents in yesteryear had somewhat different feelings about the death of a child. It was probably a psychological necessity to build appropriate defenses. Parents knew the life expectancy of children and the widespread frequency of unchecked contagion, so undoubtedly guarded their loving commitment accordingly. I often wonder if they did not feel more like modern parents do when a baby dies after only days of life, their reactions more a gentle and fatalistic sadness than the full-blown grief today's parents experience.

Though I do not advocate a return to yesterday, it is difficult for me to relate to the strange ways we have of hiding the reality of death from children. After teaching and coaching children for many years, counseling at camps and playgrounds, visiting them in hospitals and hearing their confessions, I no longer designate them by the word "children." I see them and prefer to call them "little people." I see them as compact cars instead of Cadillacs, traveling the same free ways of life, going the same places as big cars, more vulnerable and fragile to be sure, but with all parts and purposes essentially the same. Like big people, the little ones are ready and capable to talk about anything within the framework of their own experience. Often it was amazing to stop a seven-year-old in the middle of a routine confession and enjoy a richly philosophical discussion about sin, morality, eternity or death.

How easily little people can understand or learn when seen consistently as adults in miniature instead of as kids or children. The words are not important, it is the vision that needs changing. Such a rearrangement in our thinking alters our attitudes and theirs, and both of our expectations. How much better the young respond when told "Little people, time is over!" instead of "Hey, you kids, get outta here!" Even on serious matters like dying and death, little people react quite beautifully when we treat them as Volkswagen beetles instead of as Detroit's biggest. Our perceptions of little people, their needs and possibilities, often seem as maladjusted as our view of death.

During the last thirty-five years, from the inception of social security programs and their insurance offshoots, Americans removed the major traces of death from the home and family control. During the same period, we deposited most other harsh and unseemly aspects of life behind institutional doors. Except in decreasing instances, children rarely share a room with a sister who is chronically ill, a maladjusted brother or a dying grandparent. No longer do children need to understand and love the village idiot or babysit for badly retarded sisters. Middle-class home life is nearly devoid of death and crippling afflictions that make us question the worth of human life.

Despite valiant efforts to spare children from the grim aspects of life, they learn more about mortality and earlier than we realize, almost all of it in theory and in fantasy. Death abounds in nursery rhymes like "Who Shot Cock Robin?" Protestant children pray ". . . if I should die before I wake . . ." and little Catholics pray souls out of purgatory each night before insuring their own spiritual safety, in case of nocturnal death, by an act of contrition. Gone from most church programs are hell-fire preachers and brimstone teachers, only in time for Saturday cartoons to perpetuate death learning. Daddy's news programs feature a constant diet of war and tragedy. And little people like to look at dead birds, kick dead animals, talk of soldiers or grannies who died, and watch daddy trap gophers or mice. Eventually they even learn that pork chops come from dead pigs.

The greatest zeal will not protect the normally curious child. One of many mothers who sent their children out to avoid President Kennedy's funeral tells how they stopped at a furniture store window to learn what was wrong to see at home. My own studies and numerous others reveal that death and dying are emotionally laden words for children early in life. I wonder if our efforts to spare little people a harsh reality are not our own badly disguised struggle to avoid the trauma in telling. Meanwhile, our hesitation allows time and opportunity for them to sift their own data, to learn puzzling and fearful interpretations elsewhere, while concocting weird fantasies that may affect their lifelong attitudes toward mortality.

We can self-righteously blanche at the crudeness of Victorians who exposed their very young to raw and sordid details, filling their heads with verses about dead babies and the horrors of being buried alive. Is it any more enlightened or humane to leave children defenseless, poorly prepared to cope with one of life's most distressing problems?

Problems faced in discussing human death with little people are akin to those encountered in sex education. Animal sex like animal death presents little difficulty. Children are freely allowed to watch dogs mate and kittens being born. When the subject is man, we claim not to want children ignorant or frightened, nor to know too much too soon, before they are emotionally prepared. In reality, we hesitate to expose our own ignorance, fear or uneasiness on the subject of sex or death.

Three quite distinct situations arise in death education for children. First, the discussion of death with children not presently affected by death in any direct or personal way. Secondly, the discussion of death with children facing an actual or impending death in their world, maybe a relative or a neighbor. And finally, the discussion of death with children who are themselves dying. Before looking carefully at these situations, there are important considerations which apply to all three.

Any effective learning experience must take into account the world view and personal experiences of the learner. Adults tend to overlook or misinterpret the world view of little people. Most conversation about death is forced into a world of adult experience where the child is a foreigner. It is useful to reflect on some basic guidelines for understanding the capacities of children to view death.

Preschool children seem to view all death as largely a temporary departure. Even prior to age one, they begin to grasp a sense of presence and departure or absence. Notice how quite universally they respond to the coming and going in the game of peek-a-boo, almost exploding with exhilaration when they find daddy again around their tiny fingers. Soon after walking, the game grows into hide and seek, with sadness at mom's absence, joy in sudden finding.

In early preschool years, every relationship is assured of being restored. Even a daddy disappearing in divorce may return to visit, if only to fight with mom. What were formerly long absences can now be healed by telephone. Flowers and grass wilt and die only to bloom again. A dead gopher is seen running about in his look-alike. Sisters and brothers bus off to school, returning each afternoon, and mom always comes back from shopping. To attempt to force preschoolers into any other view of death is to insure their failure to grasp. Little people are limited by their experience, and in their world, people always come back.

It has been fun verifying this truth about children by watching two-year-old baby John who is living with us while his parents pack for the East. Daddy has spent two months going and coming, calling on the phone, then reappearing. And little John has expected as much. No permanent departure seemed even remotely possible.

During early years in school, youngsters begin to envision death as a person. He can be an angel of death, a monster, a Martian, a Communist or a boogey man. The imagination can picture death as a ferocious animal in human form who surprises one in the dark. Sometimes death is seen as a God who sends for men on earth. You can hear little people talk about soldiers killing enemies, police killing crooks, cowboys shooting bank robbers and spooks who wait in haunted houses to pounce.

As children personalize death, they may continue to view death as a temporary departure or they may begin to see it in the final way, as a permanent separation. Friends leave school never to return. Teachers transfer and Miss Applebaum is never seen again. Dogs die and neighbors buy a new puppy. The concept of death as a lasting separation grows at the same time that children, like most adults, revert to their earlier ways of viewing and experiencing it.

These earlier developmental stages are also sprinkled throughout adult reactions. How many survivors refuse to alter a single detail in a home where reappearance is expected at any time! Death is seen as no more than a temporary going away. Women in terminal illness confess to "seeing" illicit lovers, monsters and even animals, continually forcing them into immoral sexual encounters. Death remains a boogey man.

Death education can easily become a simple extension of a child's real world. Dealing with the child's world and experiences is so much easier in talking about death than in discussing sex. Children frequently bury dead birds, find dead rats or possums and even kill snakes and lizards, only to return to a supper table where death cannot be mentioned. And all the while their favorite television programs are likely to be full of it.

Anyone in doubt about the worth of an early and effective education about death needs only to hear the twisted ideas and emotional horrors patients in therapy recall from their earliest death-related experiences. Better still, most of us need only to search our memories. We can recapture the wonder and curiosity, the fear and reluctance, we felt in death encounters, and how painful such experiences could be if never or badly explained. Adult silence or misinterpretations left perplexity and uneasiness.

For those who insist that death education for the young is too morbid, it helps to realize again how much fear of dying is no more than the fear of living in disguise. People who cringe abnormally from pain in dying will live in forfeit of so much dynamic living for fear of painful exertion or risk. People whose excessive fear of dying includes the abhorrence of being a burden or of losing their dignity will forever avoid exciting paths in daily life where love demands being a burden at times and daring demands the occasional loss of dignity. Helping children gain an ease around death prevents the many fearful approaches to life we see in ourselves and those around us. The main purpose in openly discussing death with children is to enable them to live more freely. Our candor reduces their beginning hang-ups and helps them see death as a normal, natural, inevitable reality, a final chapter in life. The wonder and glory of life is the gist of our message, not the morbidity of death.

Any conversation with little people about death should place primary emphasis on life. After all we know practically nothing about death and little enough about life. Both are mysteries. All the philosophers who focused their mighty minds on death succeeded only in raising new and more perplexing questions. Their final answers to date hardly surpass the insights of any man on the street. Nobody knows any final answers about death beyond its inevitability. Its meaning and dynamics are slippery. Religious people may disagree until they realize the tenets of all faiths speak only about afterlife. Religion and science are locked in a partnership of ignorance when trying to unravel the mystery of man's death. Many opinions, few facts.

In any discussion with a child there can be few right or wrong answers, but many right and wrong attitudes and procedures. Children primarily need our encouragement and support. They love mystery and will readily respond to our own sense of wonderment if it has not been stifled. They quickly learn to handle the uncertainty and ambiguity about death as soon as someone permits. Already so much in the world of a child is mystery. He can live with another and final unknown, even revelling in its possibilities, if only we can.

The most worthwhile method of teaching children about death consists in allowing them to talk freely and ask their own questions, without any adult speeches or philosophic nonanswers. They need to ramble a bit, to talk a bit crudely if they wish, to change the subject and to present unanswerable questions without being squelched. The learning goes both ways. Gradually a parent knows his child's vision of the world, his views on death, his personal worries and how seriously he regards his own questions. In such free-wheeling chats, little people will unconsciously reveal their own views and fears as distinct from those we project into their thinking and feeling.

It is important for adults to be honest, no matter how undeveloped or immature their own beliefs and attitudes may appear. In families where religious belief is real and shared family-wide, religion can have its finest hour. But parents who pile their own partially believed religious solutions into little minds are only creating another Santa Claus without any assurance of an accompanying Christmas. Little people can comfortably share in big people's misgivings, in their honest efforts at searching and in the majority of their fears and doubts. The parent himself is the child's primary emotional security, not a wordy answer, a pat religious phrase or a head-patting reassurance with a sweaty palm.

Children absorb most of their death-related fears from the environment in which they live. No fearful words need be spoken out loud when latent fears haunt the house. Palliatives parents use to hush or explain fears children imbibe in every square foot of their home are useless. Words or religious beliefs may temporarily dampen tears or fright, keeping them hidden under the cover of bravado, but tears and fright remain, mutually exchanged in life's daily transactions.

In my own family home, death was always discussed and dismissed in a secure religious framework. No believing Catholic was supposed to fear death in the milieu of divine promises for an eternal happiness in heaven. But Mother and Dad were intensely apprehensive about every aspect of death except what happened in the hereafter. Dad read the obituaries, often aloud, before doing his crossword puzzle, obviously comparing ages to his own. All seven sons pretended to a religious bravado that not one of us probably felt. There was no room in our home for an admission of normal human fears and no permission for their discussion or display. Ready answers were readily available in religious terms while mysterious fears pervaded every heart.

Parents who are courageous enough to ventilate their own death-related feelings within earshot of their youngsters will discover a mutual benefit. Foremost they will learn that fears shared are fears lessened. And by their honest telling, parents grant permission to the children to be real, to feel whatever they feel, and not to be inordinately ashamed or afraid. Children should not be made scapegoats, serving as therapists to parental fears beyond their limited ability to cope. But minimal harm could flow from any open discussion of fears that are already experienced because they pervade the home. In frankness lies a basis for some alleviation of fear and for the familial endorsement of life itself.

Death education will be most effective when it becomes a part of the child's daily life. Rarely are formal sessions needed unless the child expresses or displays a need. An openness to any direction, plus a willingness and readiness to respond, are all that is necessary. Occasionally, individual children display an inordinate fear of death and a preoccupation which can be frightening. For years we saw this excessive fear in Sunday school or in catechism classes. Now we see it in the Midwest where society's overraction to tornadoes has disturbed many children. The same is true in the West with earthquakes and in the Southeast with hurricanes. We see it in every corner of the country when highly sensitive youngsters are confronted with nonexistence.

Effective parents need to spend unusual time with little ones, especially when their fears are rampant. It helps if they can repeatedly exhume their fears, chatter about them, with tons of warm holding and cuddling intermingled with ounces of answers. The best and final answer lies in the abiding security of loving folks and family in an understanding and supportive home. In this atmosphere inordinate fears will usually recede or be outgrown. Only those few whose fears are prolonged and paralyzing will need professional therapy.

The middle-class suburban American child's first brush with real death frequently comes when a pet succumbs. Deaths of animals are far easier for adults to handle. Most Americans still hold that dogs simply die and that is all. No religious concerns to perplex us, no elaborate burial rites to explain, no will to cause hidden concerns. God bless the Humane Society. Personal involvement ends with a few tears and a brief loneliness for a valued pooch. All of us are well conditioned to realize there can always be another dog. People are not so readily replaceable. We are people, and each death of our kind has more intimate effects. My experience has been that humans who translate animal deaths into para-human tragedies were not intimately involved with fellow human beings in more than a surface way.

In the face of animal deaths, we can simply explain nature's magnificent cycle. Children will readily understand and respond. They know how flowers fade and bloom again in the spring. The cat or dog becomes decrepit and kitties or puppies exchange new life for old. Only with humans and especially with ourselves does the cycle of nature become implausible. I feel unique and special. So must other human beings. And their specialness is both part and proof of my own.

When death invades the family circle, valuable opportunities arise for helping children deal with death. The Kennedy and King funerals were magnificent teaching resources. So are the fatalities of relatives, neighbors, friends or the kin of playmates.

When death becomes real, candor should be the hallmark of any effective approach. Parental fears of being too honest with little people dwindle in the realization that like ourselves, they only hear and understand what fits comfortably into their life experience. All the rest is unheard. Too much frankness or what might be characterized as carelessness will only be bypassed or digested much later.

Honesty applies more to listening than to telling. We cannot ascertain the peculiar quirks in a juvenile mind unless we permissively hear the child out. Their concerns are so different from our own. They may want to talk about worms eating buried bodies or to know if sea gulls and whales will eat grandma's ashes spread across the sea. In the next breath they may ask, "Hey, what's for supper?" Their concerns are neither orderly nor polished. Little minds flit from looking into caskets to how it feels being buried, then on to what you wear in heaven and whether dead people still give birthday presents. Some questions need answers, many do not. New questions interrupt our futile explanations as childish fantasies pour out to a permission-giving adult. The freedom to share their innermost thoughts and feelings is the important goal.

When death invades the close family circle, upsets and tears cannot be successfully hidden from the normal child. They feel the presence of something wrong. They know it. Failure to explain and to listen carefully can result in dire emotional consequences. Children can put all kinds of false and quite primitive interpretations on the shadowy data pervading a house facing death. And like kites, boogey men will rise in the winds of their ignorance.

Seldom can little people comprehend any clear differential

between their personal wishes or actions and the factual causes of human death. They can feel responsible for the death of someone they merely wished would die in a flash of anger or in a temper tantrum. When grandpa lies dying in the bedroom or in his house next door, children may take the blame for his death because they shouted or did not mind. They might infer that grandma died of loneliness because no grandchildren visited or called. Mother's constant tears after a relative's death can trigger self-blame in a child who notices mother never talks and only cries when he is near. A child's world involves cause and effect relationships adults cannot imagine unless they listen and respond honestly. Children are near puberty before they can untangle their confusion in the adult versions of causality.

Should children attend wakes, funerals or burial services? I prefer to rephrase the question since it is the wrong one to ask. Should anyone attend wakes, funerals and burial rites any longer? Little people should, in my mind, do anything big people should do, as long as they are physically able. They can handle any situation adults can handle comfortably, including viewing a deceased person in an open casket or watching while dirt is tossed over a burial vault. To attend grandma's final rites in the company of a fearful father or with a spurned and spiteful daughter-in-law would bring more harm than good to all involved. Parents who attend obsequies of any kind, going under the gun of guilt or social pressure, can expect the atmosphere to have adverse emotional effects on any child they take. The emotional tone of what is happening, far outweighs the importance of what the child does or does not see.

When little people are left at home, their environment should be emotionally supportive so they do not feel alienated from an obviously significant event in family life. They may need to grieve and mourn in youthful style, brief tears interspersed with hilarity in forgetfulness. Support is needed for their puzzlement over family happenings. They undoubtedly will need to have questions aired if not answered and to understand why they could not attend when their playmates are always attending a grandparent's funeral.

Around any grieving household, all children are entitled to their basic guarantees. First, going to a funeral or staying at home will not be blown into a big thing, never into a punishment or a clear evasion of their needs. Secondly, children will be heard and their opinions respected. Thirdly, theirs is a right to honest explanations of what is going on and why they went along or stayed at home. And finally, as much as age and maturity warrant, they will have some input into the decision to attend or to remain at home. Any experiences had within the framework of these suggestions can only serve to prosper emotional development in any normal child.

In a recent seminar, a physician whose case load regularly numbers at least a dozen dying youngsters stated without any qualification: "I do not see any purpose in telling any child the facts about his forthcoming death." Laymen and professionals took violent sides. I joined the fray in dissent. At the end of an argumentative hour, the doctor came around to the conclusion that as a general rule children should be told the truth. He endorsed the theory, but remained adamant in his practical refusal. With a tone of finality, he invited me or anyone on the affirmative who dared to begin telling his young patients on the next day's rounds. Then, almost in tears, he described some of the dying youngsters any brave volunteer would be telling. Not a single taker.

It was always simple for me to state categorically what others ought to do. As a clergyman I specialized in providing formulae for solving problems I never had to face. From my celibate throne I often told fathers and mothers of families of ten how to practice rhythm, and even more of a specialty was directing couples in their twenties how to pet without going all the way. I was never big on performance and even now tremble as I think of practicing my theories about telling a child about his death.

In my opinion, little people enjoy the same human rights as their bigger counterparts. If there is some significant benefit in their knowing about a fatal condition, they have a right to know. Clinical evidence now exists to prove that children can and will pass through the identical stages as do dying adults, if they are told the facts and permitted to discuss them. When kept in ignorance, children like adults will rarely grow beyond the initial stage of denial and isolation. Not telling deprives little people of the peace and dignity which can be theirs in the final stage of acceptance and resignation.

Clinical researchers tell us that children suffer shock and denial upon first knowledge of their condition. In their isolation they taste deep depressions bordering on despair, while intermittently experiencing rays of promise in hope. They bargain, too, with God, with doctors or favorite nurses, with parents and friends, until they reach peace in that final resignation to which their human dignity entitles them. Now that medical facts establish the emotional benefits in honesty, there can no longer be validity in questioning whether or not children ought to know.

The diagnosis of death should be made known to little people as soon as the decision is clear and final. Doctors, nurses and family obviously need delay-time to bring their own emotions under control. But no longer need youngsters die as the lonely and isolated prey to professional and parental fears or pity. No longer do doctors have the moral right to deal deceitfully with a young patient for fear of offending parents reluctant to deal with the consequences of honesty. No longer need that understandable but inhumane game be played around a dying child's bed, spoiling him rotten with toys and bribes, anything for a distraction. At last we know how to treat the dying child kindly. Knowledge is kindness, ignorance is cruel. The child is the patient, his life is being lost, his concerns are preeminent. Parental feelings are important, too. I reach out in sympathy to their fears while refusing to allow big people's needs to supersede a child's right to die in dignity and in peace.

These are strong words, maybe even harsh and autocratic. I only dare say them because medical evidence is reinforced by factors we do not know or conveniently forget about dying youngsters.

First, the dying child is no ordinary child. The ordinary process of maturing quickens through lengthy illness with confinement, suffering and deprivation. Little people who are ill for a long time usually exhibit a maturity beyond their calendar years if we peel back the spoiled exterior the adult indulgence so often creates. Sometimes dying children seem like folks in golden years wrapped in a youthful body. Sickness forced many sacrifices and much pain. They endured long hours alone, deferred much pleasure until later and underwent many humiliating experiences. Underneath, the dying child is far from that frolicking, immature and untested youngster who helps form our mental image of youth.

Secondly, children's consciences are more tender and concerned than most adults are in a position to know. Rarely do adults have a chance to confront the full glories in the bared conscience of a child. When they come close, it is too often the conscience of their own offspring, and their vision is purpled by their prejudices or limited by the child's fear of total revelation and the disappointment or rejection inherent in so great a risk.

During my priestly duties, which of course involved the regular confessional, after an hour of hearing children's routinized confessions, it was all I could do at times to stay awake. The mechanical manner we had taught them, and the sameness in the sins we had identified for them to avoid were enough to lull a saint to sleep. Often, in my unsaintly struggles to stay awake, I intervened in their rattling for a chat. It was then I learned that youthful consciences bore huge burdens seldom revealed in the ritualized way we encouraged them to seek forgiveness. Worries about daddy leaving mom, about a sister who stole from the dime store or about family fights were as common as concerns over a drinking mother, a daddy who played sex with his daughter or participation in poisoning a neighbor's cat. These and similar concerns were not on the list of sins in the prayer book. Children will play the mechanical dying game as readily as they adapted to routine confession, if adults so demand. Any game a child is taught will be played if necessary to buy endorsement and acceptance. And yet, inside his conscience the sensitive child will wrestle with unasked questions and guilt galore for what he sees happening in his own little world.

Deathbed children uninformed of their fate will often own guilt for the sadness and poorly veiled tears they witness around their bed. They can sense the phoniness in the joy nearby and can tend to believe they are being punished for something evil they did. Isolation heightens in their heavy concerns. Nobody will provide any atmosphere but one of hollow hope and artificial cheer in which the dying child must attempt to unearth what he feels inside. People nearby hug away his tears, bribe away his loneliness and bury all fears in promises for tomorrow. And perhaps the saddest of all situations occurs when a dying child learns his fate from his playmates.

Finally, children who are moderately aware and normally alert know what is predicted for them in the signs they see. They recognize their plight in memories of dying scenes on television and overhear ample evidence around the hospital. They ponder why the doctor comes so much, why dad never bawls them out, why mom looks so harried, why they cannot stay at home and why all the gifts. Their wonderment is fashioned together into a single final answer. Either a child shares what he knows about his dying or the final months and weeks become a lonely vigil, a sentence to fear and guilt, confinement and confusion.

Of the many children I visited near death, Tildy affected me the most. Burned beyond repair, her obvious pain and severe disfigurement were instrumental in keeping many friends away. I am ashamed at how frequently *I* manufactured excuses until she shared with me in our huddled confession her perplexity about how to handle her parents. This lovable nine-year-old could not tell them how much she knew and they would not tell her. Together, Tildy and I kept her secret. Only days before she died, she took my hand and said with smiling pride: "We did it, Father, we did it! I don't think they know I know!"

How do we tell a child about his dying condition? To men and women brave enough to listen, this is not a valid question. The child will do the telling if we create an atmosphere where he can make all appropriate deductions. The child's talk will flit in and out of the awful revelation, not dwelling on it morbidly, coming close to test our reactions and his risks, receding to regain hope, always making sure of no rejection, while mentally ascertaining if saying it out loud could be any worse than knowing it inside.

Who will do the telling or serve as catalyst for it? Doctor, nurse, parent, brother or sister, anybody strong and brave enough to take the consequences by being a regular visitor, a trusted confidant and a patient listener. Many adults cannot qualify. Their personal fears and latent resentment over the impending death of an allegedly innocent child prevent them from being open. They refuse to understand why this child, why my child, why any child—instead of all the used-up older people—should die. And in this adult intransigence, the needs of the child are overlooked or denied.

The consequences of not leveling with a dying child can be sad. The nicest and happiest children can be transformed into spoiled and unhappy misfits, futilely reaching out for vague tomorrows while inwardly confused and fearful at their inability to put events into any focus. In their helplessness they may lash out in disquieting vexation. Nobody will love them enough to go beyond pity and pampering to impose limitations that always before reflected care and concern. They long for the love of yesterday which was not without guidelines nor was it universal cheeriness with sadness underneath. Also, sensitive youngsters may need to finish their own affairs, make amends, repair some hurts, or even as the little Mexican boy in Tijuana recently did, leave a will under the pillow for proper distribution of his bank, his cat and his toys.

When children have known the truth about their condition, and were allowed to talk about it openly, they have been as brave as any adult. Compacts can do the same job as Cadillacs.

# 8.
# Coping
# with Tragic Death

Some mornings our daily newspaper reads like a giant obituary column for tragic and untimely deaths. Local businessmen killed in a small plane crash are brought home for burial. A wealthy matron backs her Mercedes over her four-year-old son, cradling him in her arms as he expires. An honor student celebrates her seventeenth birthday with a drug overdose, a suicide note in lipstick on her bathroom mirror. Twenty-seven miners suffocate, leaving twenty-seven widows to cope with budding families. A rookie patrolman is gunned down when he stops a car for speeding, succumbs without a goodbye to his wife and three children. A fifty-one-year-old man suffers a heart attack on the freeway, endowing his family with a law suit from the parents of five cub scouts killed by his careening car.

In each instance, if my heart is tuned in to my reading, I feel a temporary sadness. It would be so thoughtful to do something supportive for each family, maybe drop a note or mail a few dollars for some kind of fund. What do you do? What can you say? Regularly I do and say nothing beyond sending vibrations and good intentions. I convince myself there are too many, while knowing inside that it would be much the same if there were only one. Nothing leaves me more hesitant and speechless than the thought of approaching survivors of tragic or untimely death. And my research reveals my feelings are not atypical.

Even when the victims are neighbors or friends a similar paralysis sets in. All escapes and excuses are tested immediately for plausibility, any reasonable evidence will do for evasion. Never am I quite certain if guilt or friendship keeps me from running. Mentally I begin to concoct some explanations for my condolences. Every effort rings hollow, no more than words shouted into seaside winds, allowing me to keep my distance while passing time, assuring I will speak to ears when hearts are wounded.

The human heart asks only one real question when tragedy occurs. "How can I possibly undo what has been done?" The question is repeated over and over in varying forms. The mind shouts "Why?" and the heart begs for restoration. The only answer is as simple: "You can't!" And every effort at wordy consolation confirms the truth of this unacceptable reply.

Untimely death is common since rarely does any death arrive on time. Almost always too early or too late, a yesterday, a tomorrow or another year usually seems more fitting. It seems easier, though seldom easy, to accept the death of folks too old to live a fully human life much longer. When the young or unfulfilled die there is no thornless path to acceptance. And youth or fulfillment can only be measured in the eye of the bereaved. A Pope John in his seventies seemed too young and too vital to die in the judgment of his admirers.

Around untimely deaths, the air grows heavy with nervous talk and platitudes. When hearts cannot reach other hearts lips automatically move. Almost everyone contributes a quote or a comforting saying. The willingness of a silent presence coupled with hugs and handshakes never seems enough. Men resist the intimacy of love, speaking of loss in silent sorrow, so we escape into talk of banalities. With each arriving friend the litany of verbal pacifiers grows, while each placebo misses the mark, geared more to relieve the embarrassment of the explainer than to comfort the bereaved. And believers of every description, struggling for ease in an awkward situation, sometimes force their own beliefs and easy solutions on the anguished.

Religious people customarily tell how tragedy is somehow more acceptable if seen as the will of God. Untimely deaths are made to fit into his omniscient and eternal plan. Either survivors know and believe this in advance or the telling only kindles a need to lash out at a God who could will such horror on one of their own. More theological consolers refine their explanation to God's permissive will at work. God did not want but merely permitted the tragedy in his decision to create all men free, even rapists and drunk drivers. Such niceties are useful in theology classes, quite useless near death. They only serve to arouse the age-old wonder why God gave freedom to men He knew would use it so wantonly.

I recall sitting long hours with families numbed by tragedy, explaining carefully to nonhearers the intricacies of the divine cosmic plan. After a mysterious crib death took an unbaptized baby, I would fervently tell how limbo, the theoretical destiny of all unbaptized infants, was a place of natural happiness. I painted limbo as similar to earth but without pain and trouble. Still in shock or engulfed in guilt for possible neglect, parents pretended to listen, while I labored through obscure theories of how maybe the unbaptized made it to heaven after all. I gradually knew the futility in my efforts as survivors increasingly said: "Your staying and your sincerity helped more than your explanations."

When victims were older I would quote what St. Monica said while dying or read what her son, St. Augustine, wrote after her death. When the young died I would tell the awful tragedy of St. Maria Goretti who died in defense of her chastity, adding how her killer repented and was present at her official canonization. I am ashamed to say I sometimes manufactured quotes and placed them into mouths of comforting saints.

I often felt resentful and professionally put down when laymen posed their own secular or folk wisdom against my sacred comfort. "Better to have known and loved a little than never to have loved at all!" "Isn't it a shame for him to die with our streets filled with losers!" "Think of the good she accomplished instead of what remains undone!" "She had thirty-seven years while Christ had only thirty-three!" "Imagine how he would want you to react and show your true love by acting that way as a memorial."

Tender and kindly words, words borrowed from Mom, from sermons, from evangelists, words that joined my theological verbiage in only ruffling the air, dispelling momentarily the silence that shouts: "There is no answer except to turn the clock back!" Talking after tragedy is normal and human. It is useful as long as we recognize it as more parrying for personal comfort than imparting effective consolation. Try our human best, no verbal solution can salve the hurt in the early aftermath of tragic death, or for many moons thereafter.

The factor of time takes on special importance. Time alone is no healer, it can only lend perspective. Survivors relate how all sense of time disappears while they are buoyed along by a rash of mundane duties, maybe only dressing and toiletries. One solace lies ahead. One hope and one promise. Some day soon survivors will reach a hospice where they can regroup to begin life anew. Not life as it was before. Life with memories and new loves instead of with a presence that cannot be resurrected. A new life arises in promise, one tinged with nostalgic sadness, one that looms brighter with each day endured, and one made richer by the new depth of human feeling found in suffering through a tragedy. As often as I find friends who experienced some catastrophe and persevered in this struggle toward new life, I find someone uniquely able to reach out to the untouched horizons of love.

Friends of whatever standing can play important roles in the days following tragedy. Welcome friends bring the finest solace. Unwelcome friends whose presence only ignites further pain can bring new appreciation for welcome ones. The friends we depended on seeing but who come by infrequently or not at all, provide useful and safe targets for our frustration. Acquaintances can become lifelong friends, while former friends become enemies. I notice how the bereaved often make serious mistakes in judging friends too quickly in their time of need, classifying some as good, others as fair-weather.

Friends differ in their talents at consolation, offering varied profiles of strength and weakness. Only a small percentage are gifted in the art of comforting. Many friends come and display their fraternal clumsiness while others remain aloof in embarrassment. Friends hesitant to visit will despise their cowardice with a venom their critics could never imitate. They squirm in guilt, feeling shamefully disloyal.

Yet, even from behind their timidity they can beam other rays of friendliness. They may well be comforters for tomorrow when the early responders are tired of tragedy and tears. Meanwhile, they might well be lost in deeds of friendship too tiny to be noticed in tragedy, like prayers for our well-being, squelching rumors or babysitting for stronger friends who dared to come.

It is often tempting but usually unwise to suddenly rearrange the hierarchy of our friends after tragedy strikes. Friends need understanding and acceptance for their peculiar anguish. Human foibles around the tragic are discovered, not selected. There can be as much love in a tuna casserole as in a lengthy visit. Even a friend's complete failure to provide helpful support of any kind should be placed in its true perspective: Next to running from a catastrophe in our own life, the most understandable human trait to me is our reluctance to confront tragedy-afflicted friends.

The confusion that tragedy causes in survivors simulates a chorus of discordant voices, each evoking a special need. The infant inside pouts and whines for coddling. The adolescent longs to rearrange the world in a tantrum. The spineless self wants to run while the skeptic tries doubting tragedy ever occurred. The lover feels alone and wants companionship. The miser is already fretting over will and bills. The shy self wants more privacy and the bragger wants an audience. The parent pines over sibling needs and the vain self picks a dress for the funeral. All the while the guilty self hushes all strident voices.

Behind these contradicting selves stands our true and solid self. Millions have learned in tragedy how this neglected self soon stands up, stronger and tougher than ever imagined, possessed of sufficient though untried skills to cope with any human tragedy. From infancy man learns not to allow his eyes to see, his ears to hear or his mind to know more than this inner self can handle. The survivors at Hiroshima and at Dachau join survivors everywhere in testimony. Man will block what could be too much.

At the core of every person, sometimes locked unknown within this inner self, resides a set of native values that will provide meaning when all seems meaningless. I contend that within this hidden creed lies the power for each of us to become a true believer in time of tragedy. Most Americans contented in their affluence barely suspect the existence of these buried values until a catastrophe requires they be unearthed and employed.

Maybe the tenets of this buried faith are part of a religious belief long since neglected, part of a folk wisdom learned around the family hearth or traces of a scientific outlook on life learned in college. The origins or the label on the contents matter little. It only matters that survivors reach for these private treasures as soon as possible. Therein will be found their strength and true conviction, their finest consolation, the best answers to all questions and final sense to the ultimate senselessness seen in tragedy. Victor Frankl tells how he found his own hidden cache of spiritual gold in the concentration camp, allowing perseverance when despair became so tempting. It takes courage to dig so deep. It takes honesty to admit the validity of buried values and humility to live by them. Until survivors find their personal trove and empty it, they will rely on surface solutions and borrowed guidelines which can bring no more than artificial and temporary solace.

In the aura of tragedy, religious drifters may find they never did abandon their belief but grew tired of church attendance or bored by untouching ritual and sermons. Social climbers may find the futility in their search for riches and fame, choosing to return to their prior regard for beauty, simplicity and human goodness. The devout may find they never fully adhered to any religious creed when heaven or hell seem meaningless, prayer and worship pointless. When tragedy challenges our very being, threatening all purpose and meaning in life, we can if we choose learn to live by the only values that will make ultimate sense.

This is no dream or no idealistic and untested theory. I learned the contents of my own treasure trove when one of my best friends committed suicide. The two of us were locked deep in our fear of informing superiors and friends that we could not be priests any longer. When my friend chose death as preferable to candor, I realized how I treasured life and all it holds above the rejection and shame that could come from changing vocations. I learned that my religious beliefs were no more than the tip of my value iceberg. I am still discovering new values that had lingered beneath the surface for more than three decades.

Once discovered, this inner core of ingrained values becomes the source of all real and lasting recovery. It lends perspective to all that can be understood and accepted. It will not be found in fearful or hasty grasping to fill the void we feel in loss. How tempted I was to plunge wholeheartedly back into my childhood faith to find a ready answer to my friend's suicide. Our values will only finally be found by daring to experience the depths of ourselves, determined to avoid simplistic solutions or artificial sweeteners. Friends can do no more than lend direction and supplemental wisdom. Bibles and books can help, but in recovering fully from a personal tragedy, the survivor is the final source of his effective solace, his best explainer, his own most useful teacher.

Once I understood that tragedy-affected friends were endowed with such an inner power, a heavy weight was lifted. My role changed and my responsibility lessened. I felt more at ease knowing consolation could not finally come from anything special I said. I only needed to remind myself that I had never heard and in tragedy did not need an effective consolation myth. A vacuum will remain for some time, maybe partially forever. My finest role is to allow and help my friends to experience their own emptiness without running haphazardly for futile substitutes. Only new and real loves can arrest the bitter taste. My presence and support are best seen as beacons back to life anew, always confident that final recovery will be found within the self. After only days or weeks my temptation is to pull the old "buck up and pull yourself together" routine. Impatience causes me to forget that friends will "mush on" when they choose to rely on the strength they gradually find in their own reserve.

The tragedy badge can be a tempting one to wear permanently. Behind its continuing power to generate sympathy, survivors can retain and nurture their pain as an excuse for sub-par performance and irresponsibility. Family and job can be neglected with minimal loss of face. Marital tragedy provides an acceptable excuse for avoiding future intimacy with any adults. Loss of a child can be offered forever as a ticket to the avoidance of children. All such excuses seem like refusals to dig and discover the resources that can make all excuses seem flimsy.

Suicide remains among the stickiest problems for Americans to face. Official statistics count some twenty thousand suicides annually while unofficial estimates put the total at thirty thousand Americans. As frightening as suicide may be, our recent interest in studying and preventing it has fostered the illusion that suicide is far more common than it actually is. Considering the suffering and pain in our stressful world and our national love for pills and pistols, I often am amazed that suicide is not more common.

This is not to talk down to the tragic pain survivors endure after a suicide. Even before the reality of a relation's or loved one's suicide is fully absorbed by the conscious mind, the subconscious begins to fret about saving face. "How can I tell friends without degrading myself and my family?" Debbie put it succinctly in her term paper telling of finding her mother hanging in the basement. "Even before I thought to take her pulse or take her down, I was already worrying about how to announce her death without impugning her sanity or her moral soundness. I was planning a hush-hush funeral and was afraid to call the coroner or the priest. Does it run in the family? She bore me and reared me . . . like mother, like daughter?"

After a suicide, the survivors struggle within themselves over the dual problem illustrated by Coleen's plight in our discussion of grieving. Coleen was preoccupied and socially paralyzed until she could grant her mother permission to die and could endorse her mother's choice to commit suicide. These are separate tasks, neither of them easy and both of them made more difficult in the judgmental climate of our social attitudes.

The popular American mind continues to picture suicide as immoral or as a sign of severe emotional illness. I remember joking with priest friends that the only two sins we never heard in the confessional were suicide and failure to contribute to the church. Clergymen commonly did, and some still do, refuse to officiate at public funeral ceremonies for people who clearly died by their own hand. Many clergymen suggest clandestine rites, hush-hushed to prevent outsiders from believing the church endorses suicide. Such rites are deemed beneficial to innocent survivors without endorsing the crime, when in reality secretive services are generous contributors to the pain and shame of the bereaved.

With the popularity of psychology as the public explainer,

more and more Americans have learned to view suicide as an emotional or mental disorder. Somehow most of us have felt more logically and morally at ease to learn that a suicide victim was seeing a psychiatrist or was unusually withdrawn or agitated prior to the occurrence.

Recent studies of suicides complement my own observations that neither of these categorical positions is exclusively true, nor is truth found in their admixture. Sin is only committed when a man acts in violation of his personal conscience. And so much of what we label as mental illness can be only a different way of looking on life.

In the conscience of the victim, suicide can be seen at times as the only rational choice to make. An elderly professor who knew of his own fatal illness spent weeks in calmly weighing his alternatives. When he killed himself, apparently in full possession of his cool, he believed he was choosing a noble course by sparing all he loved the burden of his crippled years and the endowment of insurmountable medical bills. He did not believe that the sacred inviolability of human life was an absolute moral good as do those who brand all self-slaying as sinful. Those of us privileged to share in his deliberations thought him no more emotionally or mentally unbalanced than ourselves. Within the values important to him he was brave enough to overcome his instinct for life. As best we could observe, this man was neither a sinner nor insane. Maybe a hero—maybe a saint.

In this and similar situations, suicide demands commitment and courage. These are the two elements missing in numerous clients I have seen whose value system concluded in suicide but who preferred talking to action. Suicide can be the fruit of a tortuous ethical decision made by a moral and sane individual, surely more sensitive than most. We pay to see racing-car heroes risk their lives for cash and fame and even thrills—and inevitably a substantial number wind up in flaming wrecks. Men in war put life on the line for patriotism or for fear of resisting the draft or letting their buddies down. Martyrs risk their lives for causes and creeds that seem illusory to nonbelievers. Our narrow sense of national morality is only now widening to admit that many suicide victims are heroes, too, within their own world view, and they are more deserving of our plaudits than our shame. For many troubled persons life has become a race track and a war, even a Colosseum where the lions of conflict threaten modern men as much as Rome did any martyr. We can differ with a suicide victim about his values without indicting his final worth as an integral man.

During the heights of campus disorder in the spring of 1970, a newly graduated student doused himself in gasoline and burned himself alive not 400 yards from my office. He chose the free speech plaza in full view of hundreds of dormitory residents and dozens of passersby Our mod and enlightened campus was deluged with conflicting interpretations. Radical leaders interpreted his suicide as an heroic protest against the draft and Nixon's move into Laos. The sin-seers saw sin and the psychologically oriented saw derangement. The frightened saw no more than their own terror at the sight of a human torch and knew only the message of their shock.

Weeks later his mother and I sat for hours translating the texts of the Gregorian chants her son repeatedly played in the weeks prior to his death. The Easter Mass depicted Christ as a victim laying down his life for his beleaguered people, holocaust for sin. On the flip side the Requiem Mass, commonly chanted at funerals, promises victory over death's sting in eternal peace with Christ. Within the liturgical texts it would have been simple for me to portray the lad's death as a conscious martyrdom. Yet who could know which interpretation fell closest to truth? Within such a complexity of internal and external pressures as the boy felt, only a God could reach even an approximation of his true motives. Each human saw what his values allowed and needed.

Perhaps it is too much to hope that people bereaved by suicide can find a degree of solace in understanding the multiple possibilities of the act. They move in a daily world where the popular opinions prevail. Tranquilizers will not remove the sensation of being stared at and talked about. Their minds whirl in a circle of blaming and unanswerable questions: "Am I responsible, at least in part?" "Am I unapproachable when friends need help?" "Did I drive her to it?" "What could I have done I did not do?" And in cases where the victim had long-term problems like drink or depression, an unwelcome feeling of relief adds new dimensions to guilt and shame.

Our cruelty toward suicide survivors is more the response of a group than an individual reaction. Individuals are never as cruel about suicide as the bereaved might imagine. In general, we respond with a pity that is demeaning to survivors. Often we feel a morbid curiosity about details since suicide adds excitement and mystery to routine dying. And, close to the reality of suicide, many of us recall our own speculations about ending it all, maybe even our own attempts or near misses or those of someone dear. Then begin the rumors and the whispers, much second guessing, but seldom are these as indicative of cruelty as much as of the crudity observed in boring and bored people.

An excessive concern about the judgments of outsiders dissipates once survivors work out their own honest feelings about suicidal death, resolving their personal guilt while accepting the demise and the mode of its happening. Others are able to readily accept what we can accept ourselves. So much cruelty we believe coming from others is no more than the backlash of our own anger and resentment. In visiting survivors after a suicide, I noticed how their sense of shame and secrecy magnified my reactions of pity and morbid curiosity. When they could handle their tragedy with reasonable comfort, I found myself more able to do the same.

Already there are numerous indications of a change in society's public attitude toward suicide. Want ads and Yellow Pages in almost every major town offer a lifeline to prospective candidates. Books galore and an increasing number of suicidologists appeal to all kinds of potential victims. New funeral services designed especially for suicide victims deal almost openly with the issues survivors claim to face.

These incipient improvements within the structured church try to show respect for suicide victims as integral and moral persons, possibly overwrought beyond control or possibly no more than victims of a sensitive conscience that prized life too fully to continue living when life no longer seemed full. The ideal ceremony of the future needs to go even further, opening to everyone present an insight into the near infinite varieties of moral goodness hidden within the human person. No judgment, no need for preaching, only startling new approaches for all who are willing to face a range of complexities that in today's society we have drastically oversimplified.

Recently a friend was asked to conduct a funeral service for a minister who had ended his life in the presence of his wife and five children. Tongues wagged community-wide, with nonbelievers endorsing their disbelief while believers shamefacedly disparaged the minister's faith and hope, wondering why such a hypocrite would presume to teach "my children" about a Christ he did not follow.

My friend consulted widely in his pains to plan a proper ceremony. His theme was found in his text: "Greater love than this no man hath than that a man lay down his life for his friends." The words of the master himself. The ceremony showed convincingly how Christ's death on the cross was a voluntary surrender of his life and the constant refrain verified his route of escape. "Thinkest thou that I cannot now pray to my Father and he shall presently give me more than twelve legions of angels?" It took minimal imagination to draw a clear parallel between the voluntary deaths of minister and master.

The ceremony told without calumny or slander how the minister chose to lay down his life in Christ-like imitation for the best reasons he could know. Only the minister's motives lacked the divine quality he believed Christ's motives had. His love for Christ was enhanced instead of being impaired by his deed, at least in his own personal view. Nobody in the church knew accurately this minister's effort to spare his family and his parish from scandal. Never would he openly admit his wife's infidelity in sleeping around and the horrors of an impending divorce. He expired in his naive but sincere refusal to reject his wife or turn her into a modern Magdalene. The few worshippers who guessed the marital problems deduced enough to stop their leering. The rest of the congregation learned the dignity of a fallible man's sincerity in imitating an infallible master.

A second form of human tragedy I find extremely difficult to deal with is the death of a child who has been murdered. I will never forget the circumstances surrounding the death of Linda whose raped and naked body was found in a ditch nearly a full week after a community manhunt began. My problem was to calm her family so they would not need to avenge her death with that of the murderer. Her father and brothers ranted and raged. Friends came by to discuss retaliation. I cringed and tried to quiet everyone while feeling much of their distressing rage inside myself. The animal in me seemed to require the death of the hapless lad who had destroyed a helpless little girl.

Now I can trust more completely in the basic and innate goodness of human beings. When allowed to roam at will through their vengeful streak, venting their spleen and protesting their undaunted love, survivors gradually arrive back at the disposition that is characteristically their own. Only a few will still need revenge when their rage is expended, and all my talk and caution will not stop their retaliation. Most people will return to their normal state of gentility. No longer would I futilely try to tame a lion into a lamb. Now I would simply listen to a Linda's dad, agreeing with his need for vengeance as a normal fatherly response, all the while trusting he would shortly find within himself the values and strength to face his future.

Yesterday I argued and explained, restraining my own anger in pretense of holiness. Today I would let my anger out to encourage friends to ventilate theirs, knowing all men are more civilized once they work through anger to the reality of their hurt. Wars and retaliation always result when men have no other battlefield on which to dissipate their vengeful feelings. My sole need would be to provide an accepting atmosphere wherein the tragically grieved could recover themselves.

If someone were to assault or mutilate my wife or my daughter, I can anticipate the rage I would feel. I can imagine my need for revenge and to prove in counterviolence that I loved them as much as I feel I do. I know my temper and how my rage could be frozen. I also recognize the lamblike little boy within, a gentle person who would try to understand though unable to forget and probably unwilling to forgive. The lamb would only refuse to compound one tragedy by causing another. No great nobility in this stance, only the fruit of trying to be human for many years.

I can never forget the funeral where a man and woman were buried together with their nine children, victims of an arsonist, the jilted suitor of their oldest girl. Eleven caskets lined the center aisle in descending size. The church bulged beyond capacity, microphones and chairs outside. Many tears and constant soft sobbing, with undertone whispers about the culprit now in jail. Mutterings ranged from threats of public lashing to tar and feathers or lynching. And what would the priest say?

The priest hemmed and edged, hawed and explained, citing graphic details from the crucifixion and the ignominy accorded the martyrs in Uganda and the children in the biblical fiery furnace. Hindsight always lends fresh perspective. Now I would instead willingly risk sharing my confusion and rage, openly shedding tears buried inside. That community simmered in divisive and unfocused rage for many years. Maybe in the unity of tears and shared futility, the muting of rage in open admission, the quieting of violent plans in public discussions, a community might have joined in a search for common decency. When openly expressed in loud promises and tears, outrage dwindles into civility. Incivility only breeds what it claims to attack and prevent.

Sometimes I permit myself to reflect on all the little ones who drowned in backyard pools or suffocated in refrigerators carelessly left open. I remember tots backed over by inattentive farmers on tractors or felled by hit-and-run drivers. I recall children maimed by needless bombs and those charred in bed through the neglect of careless parents on the prowl. And all the mythology I ever heard, all the quotes from John and Paul, all the insights of Hesse and Gibran, all the folk wisdom and poetry of whatever age, join my own feeble wisdom in one grand eloquence of futility. There is no abiding answer, no consistent comfort, unless the survivor takes time to find the bricks for rebuilding within himself. God and future life soothe little more than remembrances that they might have died in a useless war. Only ambiguity and frustration are the original answers when children die in a catastrophe that could have been forestalled. Any viable and meaningful answer takes time.

Modern haste and confusion added to our affluence make us more prone to accept simplistic answers. Optimistic Americans find it difficult to walk around the rim of despair. All of us are tempted at times to reach out for the support easy answers provide and for the denial of full grief they permit. The trend is symbolized by the Jesus People who are only younger and less polished versions of a Billy Graham, able to pierce through any morass of human confusion to a simplistic Biblical answer. For me, the only possible answer for catastrophe is not a static one. It cannot be put into a newspaper column or preached in a sermon. It can only be found in man's dynamic ability to go on living, to understand his ultimate aloneness in recreating new loves, mindful of the past yet willing to reach beyond its limitations. Easy answers only decorate the lips. They deny the full scope of value one person can have for another, skipping quickly over vacuums in the heart, sloppily suturing scars of hurt, seeking substitutes where only replacements will do, cherishing the falsity in my own cheerfulness more than the truth in the profound sadness I rush to bury.

Writing an adequate letter to friends bereaved by a tragedy can be almost as difficult as visiting. Letters of sympathy take on new importance as the mobility of our life-style increases. It would be wrong to indicate that there are good and bad letters or correct and incorrect ways to console by mail. The badness and incorrectness lie more in our failure to respond to a tragedy when we know we should. Almost any letter sent is appreciated more than a sympathy card, flowers or a Mass card.

For years my desk always hid several half-finished condolence notes overdue by many weeks. My delay was for inspiration, since I needed to say something clever and memorable. I wanted neatly chiseled explanations stylized individually for each tragedy, something recipients might show to others and save for future edification. My reputation was of more concern than the grief I sought to allay. At times I was tempted to imbibe a bit to gain the unreal eloquence of booze, only I wanted my words not John Barleycorn's. My letters needed to be a production, a sermon, and hopefully a masterpiece, instead of the simple and loving tribute of one confused person writing to another.

Then tragedy suddenly invaded my own life. Letters I hoped for in floods came in trickles. Once you are the recipient of letters assuaging tragic grief, you realize that each letter bears a spirit all its own. The spirit rises above the grammar and the prose, beyond the neatness or the thought, conveying the warmth and support of a friend. The grief-stricken cannot read any more accurately than they listen. The masterpiece speaks only as lovingly as the scribbled note. Whether clumsy or preachy, I only reached out to the friend who had reached out for me. Each letter remained on my desk emanating a message I treasured, even when I disagreed with the mythology or could not interpret the words. Even the angry letters that identified myself as the culprit in my own grief spoke the love of recognition not spoken by all the half-finished or mental letters other friends did not send.

Writing to confront any tragedy means no more than sharing honest feelings. Often I bare my hesitation or confusion, offering no more than my loss for words and my supportive concern. Now that my needs to impress have lessened, I trust friends to grasp the spirit of my mood. Now before I write, I spend far more time in assuring that my mood is mine—and my words ring true—than in coining fine words or clever phrases. I could no longer imagine a greater insult to a stricken friend than sending a phony letter to soften his hurt.

There is no shame in sharing my humanity. I can share my queasiness and reluctance, even consciously leaving out those usual bits of wisdom society seems to expect. Now it is only important to send the letter before I fashion it into another means of stepping back from the clumsiness in human warmth and mutual love all friends appreciate in tragedy. The eloquence in self means far more than the eloquence of fine writing.

In retrospect, the only letter I still recall from memory after my own days in tragedy simply said: "I am your friend for good!" And it was signed with a "love" I still feel.

# 9.
# Doctors
# Near the Dying

Hidden within the mind of nearly everyone I consult is an image of an ideal physician. Men like Albert Schweitzer and Tom Dooley helped fashion it along with Dr. Kildaire, Dr. Welby and St. Luke of biblical fame. The doctor who took our tonsils out or removed our first wart joins "Ol' Doc " on *Gunsmoke* in creating our firm expectancy that physicians ought to act in a specific way. A large percentage of Americans dreamed of becoming a doctor or at least of rearing one. One entire class confessed to nurturing a fantasy idealized in white, a dedicated and noble helper, surrounded by excitement, prestige, glamor and, of course, much cash.

A hassle with an answering service late at night will temporarily tarnish the image almost as much as waiting long hours for return calls. The image fades while we idle timelessly in an outer office, paging ancient magazines, overhearing ills and expecting our name at every opening door.

Then suddenly the image glows once more in the doctor's presence, sparkling anew in his reassurance of good health. So essential are good health and mock eternity on earth that we grant almost as much deviation credit to our physicians as we formerly gave to the clergy in religion's heyday. Doctors can treat patients almost any way they choose, as long as they act legally and keep us healthy.

When terminal illness strikes our family, this latent image of expectancy affects all doctor and patient-family relations. Unless our physician can reincarnate into our image of what he ought to be, our entire faith is threatened. In crisis we require a family doc who keeps no hours, wrapped inside a scholar-scientist who knows all the best and latest treatments plus the finest consultants. We want a benign psychiatrist to unravel family perplexity and a jolly prophet for optimistic prognosis. In ordering care we want maximum skills while in paying we want minimum fees. We want a concerned man to make us feel special with computerized regularity added to a miracle worker who can reach beyond human competency. When someone close is deathly ill, we want a divine physician.

Doctors whose beat is routinely among the dying face problems little realized by most in their clientele. Much needless frustration around dying can be skirted if we better understand the doctor. Death is his ultimate professional enemy, the destroyer of all the good he has sworn to do. Behind that mask of professional calm resides a human heart which shares fully in all the death-related fears our culture harbors. The frequency of his nearness to death often serves only to improve the suavity of his protective shields without guaranteeing an ounce of improvement in expertise at openness and warmth. Each dying scene is an original. Kidneys and cancers may look and function much alike but patients and families are unique, arousing distinctive feelings and reactions. Each fresh confrontation with the dying causes new combinations in the doctor's personal feelings. Each day on his rounds he meets mementos of his own mom or dad, his grandparents, his wife or child, a former patient or a favorite friend, even of someone he intensely dislikes. Some protective device is essential when a case-load reeks heavily of dying.

In larger cities, the doctor to the dying is often a specialist, an internist or hematologist, assigned to a case when fatality is feared or shortly after its prognosis. His medical task begins when anxiety is at its zenith or when patient and family are reeling from shock and disbelief. Maybe he is requested to enact a lie or maybe he is seen as the dubious hero who discovered a cancer others missed, maybe as an enemy who pronounced the sentence of death. Seldom did the specialist know the family when life was normal, sharing only the hopeless and unpleasant side many exhibit near death. He struggles to keep a perspective by relying on his conviction that most men are lovable even when they treat him less than lovingly.

The mask of professionalism steels the doctor against death's intensity, against tears and fears, against unreasonable demands and pettiness, against any lashing out or legal threats at any tiny flaw in procedure or patient care. Masks allow for maximum concentration on medical aspects of the case, while insuring equal sharing of his medical skills. Masks preserve a portion of self for home, for private life, for friends and social or public life. To falter or tarry emotionally with even one pathetic patient can mean a loss of perspective on all others and on life.

This is the narrow path doctors to the dying attempt to walk within their consciences. To remain objective without objectifying the patient. To perform daily routines and medical rituals without loss of concern. To announce medical dogma without undue bluntness or losing listeners in mystifying jargon. To bring compassion to their role without losing competence. Ultimately, they seek to remain true to themselves without missing any human needs of patient and family.

Idealistic critics tab this professionalism a cop-out while physicians call it self-preservation and self-respect. When professionalism becomes an excuse for escaping death, it is eminently human and understandable. Few human beings I have known could become emotionally involved with more than one or two dying patients without losing balance. Even Dorothy Day whose saintliness in caring for dying patients is legend tells how the demands of a single patient can be all-consuming.

Doctors practicing medicine today have had almost no formal education and minimal special training in handling the distinctive human needs of dying patients and grieving families. Unless they have taken special pains to instruct themselves or met a rare model among their clinical instructors, they often know little more of nonmedical needs around dying than they brought from home. And what little they learned was entangled in yesterday's myth that the patient should not know his fate.

The selection process which admitted today's physicians into medical school considered two primary factors. Academic considerations were primary, grades in college, especially in science, and scores on entry exams. Secondly, decreasing attention was paid to letters of recommendation from prominent professionals while increasing attention was paid to interviews by admission committee members, usually academic physicians of the professorial type. When applicants were abundant, committee members favored young men similar to themselves, bright, hardworking and persevering, scientifically oriented or competent, dispassionate, conservative, and middle class or above. At times the prestige of the undergraduate college counted heavily. Harvard or Stanford looked better on a diploma than Los Angeles State or Western Michigan. No test or interview pretended to gauge the applicant's ability to relate to a broad range of mankind, especially to men in traumas like dying or grieving.

Early in medical school, the young men (there was always a token smattering of women) confronted the dead, many for the first time, in the unreal atmosphere of an anatomy laboratory where they practiced on cadavers. Few could grasp the emotional significance of this sudden transition from frogs or dogs to human bodies. Little effort was thought necessary to resolve emotional conflicts or to develop respectful and dignified attitudes. The atmosphere was scientific. Cadavers were viewed as scientific objects and not as the remains of someone's loved and loving friend or relative.

A few novice medics grew nauseated enough to question their continuance, but group pressure and medical machismo forced the timid and reluctant into feigned objectivity. A crudely funny humor was bantered about, kidding all nonconformers into a feeling of peculiarity for admitting quite normal reactions most humans feel around the human dead. This was the original mask donned by many medics.

While munching late-night snacks around our kitchen table, my three med-school brothers enjoyed bragging about their very own cadavers in language laymen would call crude. Mother would giggle, then blanche and leave. The tribal male in me laughed while the rest of me, sharing common genetics and rearing with my brothers, felt a vast revulsion. The medics-to-be wolfed their food, guffawing at my nibbling squeamishness, always winning the household battle for extra food, a major accomplishment in a house of seven sons.

Today's physicians learned what they learned about dying and grieving needs by observation in hospital wards. Occasional preceptors were compassionate and relaxed enough to demonstrate how to admit a patient and family into a plan for total patient care, medical and human. The more usual instructors maintained a professional aloofness, viewing themselves as pure scientists, a cut above personal involvement, leaving sympathy and fears to nurses, handholding to chaplains.

Physicians interviewed tell how few instructors modeled a role successfully combining professionalism with the pause for human investment. Only an occasional giant displayed expertise enough to walk the narrow line between objectivity and human concern, one competent and secure enough to laugh off any barbs tossed "jokingly" at too subjective an involvement.

Early in clinical rounds patterns were set for the future. Young medics adopted a style of coping with dying that fitted the least uncomfortably into their personal needs. In a matter of months they had realized how few rewards are accorded for tenderness around the death scene. At the outset, idealistic students resented a cool professionalism that saw patients as research objects, cringing inside as a medical gang of eight or ten stood over a critical patient, most quite oblivious to the patient's fright and shame. Superidealists would sneak by at night to console special patients or comfort needy families until they, too, realized fully that only scientific knowledge and the proper use of technology bring professional rewards: passing, promotion, prestige and money.

Idealists soon learned how extra involvement took a toll of time and energy. Powers needed in competitive study and practice could not be charitably squandered. Days were too short when nights were lengthened by unscheduled consolation. Undue involvement brought invectives from peers and correctives from profs, envious maybe, always garbed in manly joshing. Only the near genius was not threatened by failure or nonpromotion. Much idealism lost its glimmer when personal investment was weighed against professional advancement, and the former was the loser.

In the wake of tarnished idealism, it was easier to adapt to other traditional practices. Once futility became the diagnosis, the entire staff united in a common plan: occasional routine visits, a glimmer of hope and reporting of any fact important to medical research. Otherwise, the patient was treated with tranquilized neglect until expiration.

A second tradition was followed when death occurred. Oblige the family with facts and pleasantries, helping them to leave as quickly and quietly as possible, but not until signing a written permission for a postmortem exam. Some teaching hospitals motivated reluctant idealists by fabulous prizes for the highest percentage of signatures. Out of context these practices sound unduly calloused, but they were for many medics as much a part of training as surgery.

No wonder so many doctors adopt a standoffish role near dying, donning masks of minimal involvement while fluttering through medical rituals of fussing around. Our doctors have succeeded admirably in practicing the medical style they learned. It is difficult to criticize such success. I only regret that so many lost the art of humane medicine along their pragmatic and scientific way.

While modern physicians were learning medicine, they were losing valuable allies in the customary treatment of the dying. Family cohesion loosened in transience and divorce. Family members increasingly lost touch and regard. Neighborhoods chilled and splintered. Churches lost a personal contact with many who kept believing. Devoid of traditional helpers, the nakedness of the physician's role became more apparent.

Medical educators who see the problem believe formal courses will remedy the future doctor's deficiences around the dying. I believe it is too late. Typical medical school courses might only lecture new facts into already overburdened heads. Either medical students find time and assistance in getting in touch with personal feelings about death while mastering the distinctive skills needed near the dying, or they turn the majority of their burden over to the more skillful who are not too busy. Even when doctors know the intricate art of dealing with the dying and the grieving, the time and emotional demands of the task are prohibitive.

No longer should every physician feel obligated to do personal violence to himself by trying to deal effectively with all aspects of dying. There need be no shame in an open admission of the inability to perform a single function in human healing when modern research is opening new horizons of need near death never imagined before. So many physicians never bargained for dealing with newly realized needs in dying patients. There is no need for self-condemnation in being fearful of extensive talk about death with patients and families. In every other area of medicine, physicians identify unmet needs and employ partners or helpers when they cannot adequately perform. Not everyone is fit for psychiatry, surgery or physical therapy.

A new assistant, or better still, a partner seems required by unfolding needs and demands. For want of a better title, call him an ombudsman (or ombudswoman) for dying and grieving. He would work in cooperation with doctors, allowing them to face the realities of their practice and to do only what time, taste and talent permitted near death.

Heretofore, the finger of accusation could only indict the negligent who understood the needs near death and continued avoidance and denials. I have on my desk two current studies of large physician populations, one at a military hospital, one at a civilian. In both hospitals, less than 20 percent of the sample queried had read recent studies of dying patient needs. At a recent medical conference on dying and death, physicians were absent in droves. It would be cynically unfair to suggest that such knowledge brings no professional or financial rewards, but it is eminently fair to wonder if this reluctance to know is not as unforgiveable as the failure to respond when they do.

The physician's ignorance and unwillingness to share his responsibilities, his continued buck-passing and evasions, give the entire medical staff permission to follow the line of least resistance. And near death that line is avoidance. Nurses and aides can continue with impunity to act out their own reluctance by avoiding rooms where buzzers loudly buzz and the only disease inside is dying. This attitude infects entire hospitals where dying and grieving will never be realistically faced and handled until doctors model treatment.

To understand the several stages the dying can pass through and the insistent needs of the grieving is to realize that even the strongest and most skilled physician needs help with most of his dying patients. To pretend that the normally busy specialist is serving the full human needs of more than a handful of his patients near death is to underestimate the help the dying and grieving need. As death approaches, the patient's need to talk is interlaced with desires to be alone. Often the need is no more than for someone to sit nearby through long hours of silent acceptance. The need to talk to a confidant often arises at night, when all is still. Physicians who realize and respect these needs in all their patients know they cannot gauge or respond to them any longer.

An ombudsman partner is needed now. He would relieve the physician of all major responsibilities for dying patients and grieving families. He would necessarily be a staff and professional equal to the doctor. Otherwise he would be no more than a flunkie, paralyzed by lack of power in crisis.

Conferring regularly with patient and family, he could insure every patient who wanted one would have a confidant, while surveying moods, answering questions, relieving anxiety and skirting bureaucratic obstacles. He would not build a dynasty, no more than a few helpers at most, and the entire team would teach the hospital staff the proper stance near dying and death, hopefully resulting in destroying the need for an ombudsman. He could deal with a host of larger issues now hurriedly brushed aside, like financial concerns, family communications, decisions on transplants and prolongation of life, postmortem exams, choice of undertakers, and even the incipient stages of therapeutic grieving. He could see all visitors are properly cared for so as not to burden patient or hospital. In short, always working in tandem with the physician in charge, an ombudsman would try to infuse the entire death-related scene with a large and lasting dose of preventive medicine at its best, humane and kindly treatment.

After discussing dying in grand rounds at one of the West Coast's leading medical centers, a timid doctor came for consultation. He needed to clarify his moral posture in administering a new and life-prolonging drug to a child already bedridden for years. The parents' bankruptcy and near exhaustion, the feebleness of the child's human responses and will to live, and the draining effects on three other youngsters at home, all complicated the problem until it was overwhelming. An ombudsman was needed to share this awesome responsibility, sorting issues with them while supporting physician and parents.

Already my ombudsman sounds like a chaplain in mufti. But this doctor told of buttonholing every clergyman he could with only "ifs" and possibilities, no conclusions. The complexity of current medicine and the failure of medical ethics to keep abreast means that most ethical decisions near death can best be made by quietly sorting out what all responsible parties, especially the patient, believe to be right. In this case, parents and doctor, and possibly the patient, needed lengthy huddles the doctor felt inept to arrange or execute. Chaplains, like physicians, can only be useful when they are accepted, informed, skillful and not too busy.

The same day another physician asked for someone who could serve as confidant to his patient from out of town. The patient would not need a psychiatrist or feel comfortable with a clergyman. He was asking for the services of an ombudsman to serve or find someone who could. Several other doctors left the seminar muttering about the inanity of trying to bring peace to death. I believe they needed to chat with an ombudsman almost as much as their patients probably did.

Until you stand in the halls of a large hospital night after night, a timid and tired stranger, you might not comprehend the need for an ombudsman to help. Unless treated coldly by a doctor, the last link to life for someone you love, or brusquely by nurses who appeared indifferent to one you treasure, you will not fully comprehend how much families need an advocate, especially when death is in the offing.

Orville left his 90-acre farm to take his wife Virginia some 225 miles for hospitalization in a big city. He sold what he could and left what he couldn't. Twenty-nine weeks in a motel and without income while Virginia lingered near death. Too young for medicare and too proud for relief, Orville spent nearly seven months of aimless wandering from bedside to motel and back, not a single close friend or interested relative near, buoyed up only by the warm but rootless kindness of the everchanging nurses. Four years after Virginia's death Orville continues to pay bills that could have been reduced considerably if an ombudsman had known his plight. A simple thing like finding him a place to stay could have saved him hundreds of dollars.

A major fear in suggesting an ombudsman is that he could easily become institutionalized like other hospital employees. Already this happens where concerned administrators hire customer service representatives, lovely young ladies, to deal with patient problems devoid of any more power than their charm. An ombudsman might soon adopt in-house medical jargon, become tangled in hospital hierarchies, refusing to step on bureaucratic toes, even therapeutically. He could end up a kept man, a showpiece and pawn of the administration, unable to perform any critical task that could result in making enemies in high places.

Only a few progressive hospitals employ ombudsmen today. In the meantime, instead of dreaming about future saviors it might be wiser to learn better ways to improve doctor and patient-family relations. It helps little to seethe in resentment, praying for Marcus Welby to appear, when our primary medical contact is a scientific sphinx, or worse still, a condescending evader. Volatile reactions may ventilate the spleen but can easily result, too, in the patient's being gunned down in the caustic cross-fire. Doctors and nurses know a myriad of ways to punish hell-raising patients and families, chief of which is neglect or indifference. Patients can needlessly suffer while everyone demands that unbending personnel give a kindly concern they cannot or will not give to the dying.

Our hospitals are filled with dedicated and kindly physicians, but the cool and abrupt medic is a fact of medical life, and doubly so near death. He calls his stance professional while intimates call it personal and habitual. After years of conditioning in a medical setting, this doctor relates to everyone as peer, patient or help. His wife secretly complains of being part peer, part patient and part hired help. Children later in life realize how they were treated as patients or help. (I have sometimes wondered if doctors' children might not flock to medical school as a valiant effort to achieve peer status with an admirable but busy dad.) At home or on duty this hyper-professional remains emotionally aloof, talking down to all but doctors, prescribing, ordering, diagnosing, keeping everyone waiting. His practice comes first, even before his patients. Until such men come to grips with their stilted style of relating to others, all our frustration and resentment only forces them further into their rigid resistance, a professional mask.

Outside of a few impossible cases, relations can be improved by either side. A doctor friend, troubled for years by his inability to relate openly to dying and grieving people, tells how he learned a whole new approach by helping Carey, a victim of leukemia. From the day of diagnosis Carey demanded straight shooting and he scoured books and journals until he knew almost as much about his fatal condition as most physicians. He knew the drugs currently in use, their possible combinations, probable side effects and expected terms of usefulness. And his wife and family knew almost as much.

Carey became a peer with his doctor. Together they consulted on new symptoms, decided new prescriptions and shared equal responsibility for each remission or exacerbation. Fraternal warmth grew in this peer alliance and once again, like it was in years gone by, death became a total family affair. In Carey's room, the doctor always knew what to say without useless ritual. Phone calls often saved visits and this full involvement brought peace to all parties.

Today, reasonably well-educated persons who accept their prognosis could, if encouraged, approximate Carey's manner of facing death. Death could bring learning and purpose to everyone involved. With the abundance of biological and medical interest in our modern world, doctors need not remain imprisoned in their role of wizard, hoarding arcane secrets from educable patients and families. If families of yesterday could apply folk remedies, embalm, casket and bury their dead, modern families can learn to be emotionally involved in their dying. In this optimal atmosphere of sharing, other important decisions could be facilitated. Problems involved in transplanting, autopsies, extending life by machines, and euthanasia, all those decisions now reserved for medical and patientless caucuses, could be faced squarely by those most intimately involved— patient, family and physician.

Experienced students in classes on dying have noted another way to improve relations with difficult physicians. They suggest that at some early stage in fatal illness, families convince the doctor that they, too, are his patients, and need his professional help. Nurses have told how they broke down the barriers of the most aloof and frigid doctors they knew in the hospital by approaching them as patients. In a term paper for my thanatology class, a widower told how he utilized this technique. After freezing in the chilly atmosphere his wife's doctor created, he brought warmth to her deathbed scene by visiting the doctor in his office. He requested help for his grieving and his recurrent colitis that it probably caused. Thereafter, there was something real to discuss, curable symptoms instead of only dying. And new friendliness grew.

Concerned physicians need new tools to solidify relations with difficult patients or families, too, especially when facing the prolonged dying seldom studied in school and more rarely faced in yesterday's practice. It helps if they can cease to see the dying as dead. The less useful and productive patients really are, the greater their felt need to be both. A doctor can improve many difficult situations by capitalizing on this need, asking patients and families to help him by doing anything from recording reflections, to helping him understand others better, to knitting a pair of booties for his granddaughter. He can seek prayers from praying patients, pictures from artistic ones and recorded suggestions from complainers. A few moments of inventiveness can result in weeks and months of additional peace. The more a physician can trigger this usefulness by friendly requests, the more fulfilled the patient becomes and the less reliant on drugs. Similar requests can do much to lift the hopelessness of the family as well.

As a last resort, a third party may need to thaw the iciness in relations. Someone with a fresh perspective can often succeed in taking the physician as he truly is, enabling the full and productive use of his skills, helping his guard grow down. As families recognize his skills and respect the frailty of his resistance near death, even the most rigid physician will soften. They need a face-saving assurance that bystanders appreciate their role and are upset friends instead of super critical know-it-alls or legal adversaries. Then they may dare become as warm as they can.

To me, the most perplexing problem near death is the decision whether to prolong the life of a dying patient. The theoretical arguments we hear can be stimulating and logically satisfying, but when your mom or dad is writhing in unbearable pain with no hope of respite, or lingering unconscious beyond hope for normal existence ever again, what do you suggest? What would you suggest if you were so involved?

For years I taught courses to college students about medical ethics without fully understanding the total problem until I watched a doctor stop the life-saving machines on a nineteen-year-old girl. Suddenly, logic interlaced with emotion and an awful sense of responsibility. The machines had whirred for ten days, then no brain waves, no promise of any normal life, ever. I heard myself explaining the ethics. I heard a tear-drained mother and a weary father concur with a doctor. We all agreed, but I still felt like a little God crossbred with a hero and an executioner.

Currently there are three ethical positions on the prolongation of life. The first view is ethically easiest since it involves no decisions. Everything possible must be done to prolong any degree of human life by every known means, because life is inviolably sacred, even wispy and useless or uneven strands of it. Advocates of this extreme position believe that life is an absolute good, the supreme gift to man from God, and man is obligated to defend it with every human invention, drugs, machines or transfusions, until no further life is possible.

This first view is often mocked by the more liberal but can become tempting even to its staunchest opponents when a loved one is living artificially by grace of a machine. Who unplugs the machine? Rationally it is easy to decide until primitive emotions cloud reason and we allow strangers to do what we guiltily realize is our ethical choice.

The second position holds that no extraordinary means need be taken to prolong human life. Ordinary and usual care or techniques are all that is required. In this view, life is indeed a blessing but cannot become a supreme good to be preferred above all others. The complexity of this position rests in making the rational judgment between ordinary and extraordinary procedures or techniques. Care that is extraordinary in a small southern hospital is ordinary at Mayo Brothers' Clinic. What is usual care in the southern hospital could be unusual care in a small ship at sea or in the Vietnam jungles. Among the poor who cannot pay or are not subsidized, ordinary and usual means will differ markedly from those applied to the well insured or wealthy, though I wish they did not.

How do advocates of this view distinguish ordinary means from extraordinary? They say any such judgment must bring into perspective all factors in the personal, familial and community situation: the age and life expectancy of the patient, the financial picture, the quality of life being preserved, the needs of others to use the heart or lung machines, or the availability of surgery or more competent consultants. These are only some indicators of all the ethical factors to be considered.

When an indigent and senile woman of seventy-eight years requires surgery for a brain tumor, this would be extraordinary means. The same operation would be ordinary means for a healthy mother of four. The use of a heart or lung machine would be ordinary for a ten-year-old in a university hospital, but extraordinary means for the same lad in an African bush hospital. All the ethical factors are carefully weighed by all important people involved, patient, doctor, nearest of kin. In essence, the thrust is toward doing the best we can with all the resources at our immediate disposal.

In the many situations ordinary care cannot be clearly distinguished from the unusual, the nod is always given to the prolongation of life until the issues can be clarified.

Advocates of this position do not see themselves as hairsplitters, convinced rather that there is a distinct difference between killing someone and allowing nature to take its course toward dignified death. The wily question remains. When do you cease transfusing, pumping, massaging or substituting? The point is theoretically clear. Never before all concerned are convinced that there is no further viable possibility of normal life beyond vegetative survival. How is it done? By neglecting to continue medications or supports which artificially serve to keep the patient alive. We simply allow nature to take its course. Now that machines and drugs to prolong life far outstrip our ability to help men use and enjoy the life they keep, this position makes some sense to the majority of people.

The third position, euthanasia, makes increasing sense to many. In this view a lethal drug is administered to cause death when the continuance of life seems intolerable to the decision-makers. Conscious patients concur in their own demise, even administering the dosage at times. Unconscious patients are terminated by their own prior consent, or by the unilateral decision of physician, nurse or relatives, often in caucus. Extremists believe this active intervention can happen as early after the diagnosis of death as the patient deems feasible. More modified views insist that death should only be caused when pain becomes intolerable or when vegetative life is the only promise for the near future.

Critics of euthanasia claim it resurrects the views of Hitler in his treatment of the Jews, disposing of whatever is no longer useful or productive in our society. Louder critics see advocates of this view as playing God-games with human life, opening the door to political intrigue and social vendettas in disposing of enemies. Children could dispose of unwanted parents, the Mafia would have an easier way to wipe out opponents, and the entire fabric of doctor-patient relationships would become frayed with suspicion and mistrust.

To advocates of euthanasia, all such responses sound hysterical, wildly denying what seems to them as the ultimate in free and dignified choice. Man, they say, controls his own destiny and does not passively await the destruction of all he holds dear in self and others. It is intelligent action and not the futile reaction of a dumb animal. It is man courageously rising above his ignoble fears to rationally free himself from the agony and derision of undignified and painful death. The decisions could be made peacefully and without as much intrigue as critics suggest, perhaps in court, in caucuses of doctors and families, in countless safe and respectful ways. The strongest argument made for the legality of this third view is the frequency with which active intervention is being practiced in hospitals, homes and old-age institutions.

Increasingly we hear whispered admissions of active cooperation by nurses in old-age homes, by physicians, orderlies and aides. Some seem guilty about their complicity, others feel heroic, still others quite stoic. It is easy to understand this posture if you regularly visit a home for the elderly or a large and lonely medical ward in a big city hospital. It is easier to understand, too, if you hear a recently bereaved widow tell about her months of witnessing unbearable pain, of her struggles to sedate her dying spouse without causing addiction, of her shock at repeated indignity and about her fears of rocketing costs to keep the skeleton of one she loved alive.

Spectators can find idealistic fuel for arguing their own position in any of these views. But so long as we defer decisions until actual dying scenes cloud our judgment with pain and pity, weariness and hopelessness, decisions will be made expediently with minimal regard for patient rights and choices or for our own personal ethics. Numerous Americans near deathbed scenes are already doing what they believe is right. Laws that permitted each man to act as he believed would alleviate much guilt, shame and furtive secrecy. Doctors and nurses could tell their practices out loud. The guilt and fear of illegality would not be added to what is already an overwhelming burden.

The patient ought to have the essential say long before impossible pain and exhausting suffering interfere with his rational and ethical judgment. I suppose any suggestions about prior decisions deposited in a will or in the memory of loved ones would be about as wasted as advocating preselection of an undertaker or planning a funeral in advance. Survivors often rebel and do what they personally wish.

For me, I hereby give my wife and my doctor full permission to make any decision that seems sensible to them when I can no longer resist or care. Meanwhile, I will make all decisions myself. And I know, as best a nondying man can, that I do not want extraordinary measures to interfere with my dignity and peace in dying.

Physicians tell of wondering what their role should be when a patient dies. After immediate expressions of sympathy, should they send flowers, a note of condolence or attend the funeral? Should they visit the family later as a friend? Many doctors simply say a not too certain "no" to all options. There are many reasons given. Time is too precious, emotions cannot take such frequent contact with mourning, and presence only pricks and prolongs memories of dying and death.

In a wide survey of recently bereaved people, few expected

anything more from their physician after death. His contract terminates appreciatively at death with no further contact anticipated. A few told how the doctor's presence restricted their discussion, so best if he fades away. Others told how their family resorted to a therapeutic shadowboxing with their absent doctor, jabbing his manner and style, refereeing his decisions, judging his bills and even partially blaming him for the final fall. A doctor's continuing and unusual kindness might be misinterpreted by those who need to second-guess his worth, while absence is readily understood by those who have nothing but undying gratitude.

Undoubtedly, it seems silly to those who admire and love their doctor as I do mine, or to those who had good experiences with a doctor through dying days, to write such simplistic things about professional men. It is not.

At a recent convention for California Funeral Directors, a physician member of our panel suggested that the 275 funeral directors begin to call family doctors after death to inquire about special problems mourners might be facing. He recommended new teamwork in facilitating therapeutic grieving. The funeral directors nearly laughed him out of the room in mock derision. To a man they told of the rudeness they had experienced from physicians, the disdain, the coldness and evasion. They told of repeatedly calling or of waiting like puppies in an outer office for a doctor too busy to sign a death certificate. Only a single positive statement was made about any physician's concern for survivors through the grieving period, and that was about the speaker. At death, it appears that most doctors' involvement ceases even when they could easily impart information that would assist grieving families.

As a retired pre-med advisor and occasional counselor to medical students, I watch so many future physicians grasping greedily for grades in the competitive madness that is pre-med and medical education. And as I inspect the processes for admission to medical schools, I can see the underlying mechanics so clearly, that I can forecast that without a humanistic revolution, the treatment of the dying and grieving could remain little improved for many years.

When I heard President Nixon's physician acclaim little known acupuncture as a superior form of anesthesia to the ones we know, I secretly hoped we might soon discover a new humanistic approach to death superior to that now widely practiced. There are signs of hope. Medical schools increasingly offer programs on thanatology and humane treatment of grief. Medical students with sensitive social consciences clamor for larger doses of humanism to purge away the crustiness of greed, impersonalism and arrogance they abhor in some of their future peers. And in many places, doctors are awakening to new interest in death-related problems.

Until these seeds bear fruit, I would no more expect the average physician to impart death education than I would have expected him to teach my child about sex when his own sexual education was limited to anatomy. Reformers are on the move toward a people-oriented medicine without losing the magnificence of the science we all admire.

# 10.
# Reflections
# on Funerals

Not long ago I attended a funeral of incredible ugliness. The minister kept referring to the deceased by the wrong name, totally unaware of frantic cues from the pews, mistaking our winces and near groans for tears of muffled grief. The eulogy by this insensitive last-minute hireling had obviously been canned for any occasion. His suavity hinted he could be speaking to any luncheon club anywhere, except for his rude and impertinent insistence on forcing his religious assumptions on the semireligious friends of a dead nonbeliever.

I wondered then and still wonder what purpose such a funeral was thought to serve. Who needed it? Nearly everyone departed in humiliation and anger, pitying the family too distraught to accept our sympathies. I wondered about that man of God who could be paid to talk so glibly about death without touching a single unifying spark in his saddened congregation beyond anger for himself. I wondered why the family needed this hollow and decrepit ritual and why anyone allowed them to put themselves through such a travesty after six months of watching their daughter die.

Fortunately few funerals compare to this one. Most successful modern funerals could at best be termed inoffensive. Recently I attended a truly beautiful ceremony where warmth and meaning permeated saddened hearts. Obvious care had insured that all would grow nearer to each other around the memory of one they had known along different paths. No bragging or boasting, no canonizing of a saint, only realistic word-pictures that ignited a truth spark in each of us. Prayers for the praying kind in silence that allowed freedom for nonbelievers to offer their own spiritual tribute. The deceased's God was introduced lovingly without violence to individual differences. People chatted amiably as they left, sharing fond memories now crystallized, saddened but refreshed and uplifted, encouraged to renew life without an important friend.

Perhaps, I remember ugly funerals more than uplifting ones because ugliness is on the rise. Or it could be that I expect the funerals for all my friends to be beautiful and refuse to believe this is too much to ask. If funerals fail to inspire and unite, maybe they have lost their purpose.

Increasingly people are questioning the reasons for continuing customary funeral practices. You may not hear the questions since reform of funerals hardly ranks as a fit topic for polite conversation. They wonder if traditional funerals are necessary now that life has changed so drastically. What purpose do they serve? Can funerals be meaningful where families are less intimate, close friends are fewer and neighbors are often strangers? Are most funerals only vestiges of our small town or neighborhood heritage. our immigrant cultures, our parochial churches and our former style of family life?

First, let's be clear about yesterday's funerals. Not all or even most were meaningful and beautiful. Much talk about the joy at Irish wakes or the warmth at Polish or Italian funerals is only nostalgic and inventive talk. Many I attended as a boy and as a clergyman were only larger and longer versions of the chilling and sordid rites I resent today.

I remember dozens of funerals where solemn rituals cloaked the fact that the Reverend Father did not know who was in the casket or the pews. Often dutiful undertakers would brief the celebrant five minutes before the ceremony. In Latin chants priests often prayed for "he" when "she" was in the casket. Unintelligible rituals hid much sham and cold disinterest from mourners, as did the church's insistence that nothing personal be said. Eulogies were outlawed.

I attended wakes and post-funeral feasts where crowds of relatives and friends seemed united in reverent sorrow. Beneath the surface I saw intramural squabbles, legal proceedings brewing, arguments about wills or whose turn to pay, and who should have kept dad during his dying days. In all the world there is no fight like a funeral fight. Outsiders could see beauty in the outer facade, abundant tears, trips from afar, scores of comforters, when so often the beleaguered bereaved wanted only to run and scream, relieved beyond words when "comforting" was finished. Often only muted motives and pious words kept an appearance of family unity.

What human purposes are funerals supposed to serve? Reviewing man's funeral practices through history and in other cultures, the purposes seem quite consistent and clear. First, the human body grown quickly ugly in death needs to be disposed of in a legal, sanitary and reverent manner.

Secondly, funeral rites terminate officially the earthly life of the deceased while affirming the solidarity of the community left behind. The role of the dead individual changes from one of living influence to one of memory. And finally, funeral rites assist the bereaved to accept the death and to begin life anew without the deceased.

Anthropologists find these three purposes forming a common denominator for funeral practices in all but a few cultures. Particular cultures with varying views of this world or of a life after death exhibit a host of distinctive practices. Some nations fear that dead spirits will haunt and plague survivors. Catholics believe most souls to be imprisoned in purgatory and funeral prayers will assist them heavenward. Some cultures have insisted that deposits of money or food, in some cases even wives and servants, be interred with dead men for sustenance and companionship in the beyond. Often funerals have included human or animal sacrifices to placate an angry or an indifferent god.

Radical reformers would be unwise to discount the importance of funerals for other reasons than historical. Numerous philsosphers and statesmen have maintained that the mode of burial is an accurate measure of the quality of civilization flourishing among a nation's people. Gladstone said it as clearly as anyone. "Show me the manner in which a nation or a community cares for its dead and I will measure with mathematical exactness the tender sympathies of its people, their respect for the laws of the land and their loyalty to high ideals." Such an overstatement might lead us to believe federal monies could better be spent on funeral reform than on law and order, but there is more than a kernel of truth in such views.

One can rightly wonder about radical reformers who debunk all funerals. Love so easily and quickly terminated is highly suspect. Those whose friendships can be instantly snipped off, all mementos quickly junked or destroyed, seem as strangely inhuman as those whose funeral rites deify the dead and adore dead bodies. History and experience laugh at men who claim there is a right or wrong way to bury or memorialize. Every institutional approach whether among ancient Indians or modern secularists can be rife with superstition or rich with beauty and meaning. Our single concern is to bury our own dead in a truly humane fashion that respects our dead, ourselves and our community of friends, without adding undue burdens of grief and cost.

Prior to looking at the purposes funerals can serve in our present culture, it helps to realize that much of our loud griping about funerals, our indictments and facile solutions especially when we are not involved, could be only further signs of our national unwillingness to confront the stark reality of death. Avoiding funerals that promise ghastliness, castigating morticians as ghoulish monsters who prey upon grief, scorning organized religions for their inability to make funerals relevant—all can be so many tons of sour grapes. Our outspoken complaints can be rationalizations for not wanting to be near a human corpse. Nobody realizes this possibility more than I. No matter their beauty, I intensely dislike all funerals until they are over. Once present, the dislike is lessened by any inspiration, but beforehand I am tempted by any excuse to stay away. I encourage effective and beautiful funerals only because many funerals are a must.

Not often will you hear objections registered against funerals as legal, sanitary and reverent ways to dispose of a body. When life leaves, decomposition is swift. Odors and even contamination may follow. For many years we have delegated this unpleasant task to undertakers. Previously, and still in more earthy or poorer cultures, the task of disposition belongs to family and friends. Even small children join in bathing, embalming and dressing grandpa or a baby sister. Willingly, if complainingly, we allow undertakers to make a living from this now unseemly work. Rarely will you hear those who are not undertakers envy this portion of the undertaking task. The only pleas are for lower costs and for more options than embalming, casket and burial or cremation.

It is impossible to envision how the corpse could be handled by other than professionals in modern life. Our tastes and living habits make homes unlikely places for such activities. Churches once talked of providing this service but seem now to be moving to more ethereal and social concerns. All over America new crematoriums are rising. Currently their proprietors work with funeral directors, but gradually plan to work around them, offering body preparation and cremation plus disposition of the ashes for less than two hundred dollars.

A near unanimous national complaint by critics of the undertaking profession is that they will not offer more options. Although this complaint is rarely true, the image perdures with a corresponding fear that traditional undertakers will always insist on embalming, improving and casketing every body, even when cremation is to follow at once. The truth is that enlightened professional funeral directors will permit almost any combination of options, willing to gain and maintain community respect and regard even while maybe losing money. Short-sighted and panicky morticians cause the illusory image to remain, still pretending that laws or health codes require services and equipment not required at all.

At least one professional funeral director in every town cooperates with memorial societies burgeoning in more populated areas. Memorial societies are nonprofit cooperatives that use group bargaining power to obtain for their members inexpensive funeral rites, any combination of equipment, services or rites tailored to individual needs. Membership can be as low as a few dollars and can be obtained before or at the time of death. An entire funeral package can cost as low as one hundred and fifty dollars, as compared to the hundreds and even thousands of dollars people can and do pay for traditional rites.

The second purpose our funerals should serve is to terminate officially the life of the deceased, transferring his societal impact from living influence to loving memory, while affirming the solidarity of the community he left behind. During the several days between death and funeral the many lives of the deceased are brought to a close. The will is read and replaces his voice as directive of his affairs. No hospital to visit. Maybe an empty place at table, a bed not slept in, a vacant chair near the television. Credit cards are cancelled, insurance collected, bank accounts changed. To physical death is added absence from office or church, from club, old-age home or neighborhood. The funeral becomes the focal point for private and public pronouncement of one life's cessation answered by each community's affirmation that life will continue one member short.

Frequently this second purpose of funerals has lost its importance outside small towns or tightly knit neighborhoods, especially when families are small. The lonely and the isolated in our society die to their community long before they are physically dead. The abandoned old and mentally ill are buried in institutions long before death. For the friendless, public funerals do little more than mock their plight aloud.

How clearly I remember burying the elderly denizens of

city jungles when not a single friend would come to mourn. A kindly captain from the Volunteers of America would find them dead in a pauper's bed. Together we would reenact a solemn ritual, as dignified as any king's except for lack of congregation. To a chaplain at a county home for the aged, death often revealed that there were no relatives or friends to notify. Strangers for pallbearers, no one for tears, a taxpayer's burden whose final shame was to have a friendless funeral stared at by idle gravediggers waiting to cover that shame with a more friendly earth.

Where family and community ties are strong, the funeral can reflect memories that bind people together in new unity around a treasured loss. Families can be refreshed in renewed appreciation for parents and each other. Schools can gain new spirit in common allegiance to a dead teacher or student. Neighborhoods can gain new zest and respect for the humane treatment of each other in the loss of a common "Uncle Ed" or "Grandma" who gave every kid a cookie. Even a nation can know new resolve and purpose around the bier of a young president.

When there is no one to mourn meaningfully, no solidarity to be reaffirmed, no memories to be prolonged, this second purpose of funeral rites is not fulfilled. Private disposition would seem more dignified and respectful. No need to broadcast the loneliness or lost importance of one we loved.

This is not to say small funerals cannot be beautiful. One time I arrived to conduct a funeral for an elegant lady who died in the county home. Only five fellow patients and a nurse were in attendance. Not one of us had known her for more than the last four of her ninety-two years. No ritual seemed to fit. Instead we pulled our chairs into a circle near the casket and each told recollections of our friend. The jokes she told and the tricks she played were cited as commonly as her virtues and human foibles. Laughter mingled with tears united us in affirming our own hold on life and our determination to make the county home a happier place to live and to die.

The third purpose funerals can serve is to help the survivors accept the reality of death, assuaging their grief, while moving toward a new beginning without someone near. A well-handled funeral can contribute healthily toward effective grief therapy. An ugly funeral serves little more than to deepen the pain of loss in shame, deferring the grieving process or unduly prolonging it.

Funerals require decisions. Shock and usual disorganization are overcome or pushed aside in the need for instant conclusions. Choose an undertaker, grant an autopsy, select a casket, pick out clothes, open or closed casket, buy a grave or an urn for ashes. Undertakers are helpful but grievers need to decide on pallbearers, newspaper announcements, relatives to inform, clergy to officiate, flowers or causes for memorial contributions, reading the will, finding valuable papers, finding places for friends to stay.

As plans proceed condolences pour in, notes, flowers, phone calls, visitors, offers of assistance. Gratitude is intertwined with grief. Talking and planning unwind resistance and the sight of casket or body can hammer home reality. Friends join mere acquaintances in reaching out. Someone is gone but many others are here. The planning and the funeral rites can lend a finality and a reality not found in private or secluded ceremonies, even though they take more of an emotional toll than the inexperienced could realize. During a well-planned and beautiful funeral, the grieving process takes one giant step towards completion.

This third function of funeral rites can be indescribably painful and even emotionally harmful in the aftermath of a lingering death. A public wake and funeral can force those who already completed their grieving to resume a posture of grief to fulfill the needs of relatives and friends. A dead husband's mother will hardly understand a tearless widow when she flies in from out of town to mourn her son.

New guilt affects an overgrieved heart. The widow or widower feels it for not summoning tears spent months before. Children wonder if they are calloused or unloving when unable to shed tears they do not feel after watching long weeks of suffering. Now that lingering deaths are so common, more public permission from friends and relatives is needed for quick and private disposition of those who in all but a breathing sense died long before their funeral. They had their wake on their deathbed, grieving, tears, sadness. Their funeral was held repeatedly as visitors came to acknowledge their gradual death. The bereaved will rarely dare hurry through burial and on to new life, unless those near understand and encourage it. Ours is the first society to face lingering deaths in such proportions. Too long have we deferred the innovations in funeral customs that could humanize the aftermath of slow and tortuous dying.

To the extent that any funeral fulfills all three purposes, it is an effective funeral, human, meaningful and worthwhile. Failure to fulfill any one of these three purposes means the funeral was poorly designed and lacking in purpose. A funeral becomes beautiful as it adds to these purposes a lasting inspiration, unusual avenues to new peace and meaning plus exceptional help in therapeutic grief. Each segment of a beautiful funeral needs careful design to fit the needs and sensibilities of the deceased and as many friends as possible.

For the inexperienced, certain funeral practices can be troublesome out of proportion to their importance. The purchase of a casket has been the most traumatic for many.

In addition to wading through carefully engineered merchandising schemes some funeral directors continue to employ, the bereaved tell of overwhelming value conflicts. They recall the deceased's insistence that "any old pine box will do." Never have I heard a friend request a bronze casket in advance. As shopping progresses, the bereaved prehear relatives scolding their skimpiness, indicting their greed, and all the while self-guilt whispers within: "Nothing is too good for him!"

No time for consideration or study of the budget, while maybe a little burial insurance inflates the purchaser's sense of wealth. It is so easy now to say what we would do then, but when all the factors in loss and grief combine with guilt, social pressure and a press for time inside a tired mind, regrettable decisions can easily result. This alone is argument enough for predeath planning by those brave enough to apply. But even preplanners tell how when grief and social pressure are real, they are never sure they should not upgrade.

Many recommend the consultation of an objective third party though funeral directors often see this as an intrusion into a professional relationship, a trespasser on privacy who can never understand the entire picture. My experience reveals more than a little truth in the undertaker's argument. When asked to accompany grievers or when volunteering, I felt a need to be protective, almost a hero, sometimes preventing grievers from splurging a bit to fulfill their deepest needs. Whether I like it or not, expensive funerals are one way the economically oriented have for relieving some guilt. Afterwards my role was sometimes resented, my decisions questioned and all mistakes laid on me. Neither funeral director nor family was happy, nor was I.

The argument by the funeral directors against third parties

often contains a falsity, since an important point is not revealed. An objectively compassionate third party is too impartial to be swayed by those peculiar human feelings that make people plunge into funerals they cannot afford.

When funeral directors resent the intrusive heroics of outsiders, it is understandable. No matter how generous or kind they may personally be, funeral directors are not philanthropists to the bereaved of America. They are primarily businessmen with massive overheads. Each burial service reminds them of the huge investment their plant, personnel and equipment represent, undertaken on the assumption Americans will always want to be buried the way they were in yesteryear.

When seen in perspective, funeral directors are highly mannered and neatly manicured merchants, steeled by economic necessity and professional experience against any but surface involvement. Their mild and sympathetic approach is at once their sales pitch and their human shield against too great an investment of self in any one death. Other professionals are allowed their masks and I am allowed mine. Our frequent mistake is to expect too much, failing to take the average funeral director for what he truly is: a moderately well-educated, highly motivated, efficient businessman, with a wealth of skill and experience in areas we find unfamiliar or scary. And of all the service people in our society who allegedly overcharged for their services, like doctors and plumbers for example, I find morticians to be the kindest, the most helpful and certainly the most available.

The only time I cannot accept the mortician's point of view is when I meet a schemer. Schemers hawk bronze caskets and overpriced vaults, trafficking on grief, using high-pressure methods with low-pressure façades, allowing survivors to believe useless trappings are required by law. There are still more than a few devious and hardened schemers in the ranks, despite the best efforts of responsible men and professional societies to weed them out. Ethical morticians speak of scheming colleagues with more vehemence than I dare. I only know they continue to heighten guilt and fear by every gimmick and fraudulent technique, exploiting the bereaved with no more humane feelings than I have for this brand of mortician.

With a truly professional funeral director no third party is necessary. No fear of being robbed or misled need afflict an already overburdened mind. He will do whatever grievers truly want and will take time to find out their desires. His business future rests on a sterling reputation and he will not jeopardize his integrity for a few silver coins. The commission mongers from high-pressure mortuaries, the fly-by-nights, the svelte advertisers all scare me. If it is not too morbid to consider, it pays to pick a mortician in advance. I already know mine.

Even among the experienced we hear discordant opinions about the wisdom of viewing the body. You can hear viewing proclaimed as the sagest of choices, making death seem real and less mysterious, dispelling folk fears and spookiness. Or you hear it damned as destructive of every beautiful and lasting memory, tarnishing every recollection with the image of a ghastly and haunting face.

There cannot be any wrong or right answer on viewing. Personal taste, custom and freedom of choice are paramount factors in deciding. Skilled morticians are usually adept at explaining why people open or close a casket. In the hands of such expertise, even the bereaved too crippled to care or to choose will at least live with the conviction they were told the difference.

When the body is not to be shown, considerable time and

expense could be saved in cosmetics. Funeral directors know how people change their minds and believe they are warranted to perform identical cosmetics for open or closed casket funerals, unless they have absolute assurance plans will not be switched.

When death occurs suddenly or far away, viewing the casket, open or closed, can teach death's reality. Mourners who were deprived or chose not to see even the closed casket, tell of difficulties in realizing the factual nature of death. I cannot object to those who desire to remain in their illusions, blocking the entire affair as a bad dream. I can only sympathize with their refusal to grow out of former loves into new ones. I can realize the pain in worshipping the past, avoiding the present and the future, while deferring any hope for reestablishment.

Funeral directors find the open casket is becoming less popular. Is this a more civilized approach as some believe, or another evasion? After prolonged dying or when disfigurement occurs in dying, it seems to me the grossest of indignities to allow public viewing. After sudden death the body can look almost alive. Friends tell of benefits gained in long periods of staring, even in touches or kisses, while others find such excesses abhorrent.

I remember one night shortly prior to my decision to leave the priesthood. Trying mightily to face my own mortality, I sat through most of the night in the presence of a dead friend's body being waked. Candles flickered eerily, a few stragglers broke the ominous silence, but hours of meditative staring failed in making death or life any more real than before.

Nobody ought to be forced or pressured to make a decision about funeral conduct, especially the young or emotionally unstable. The psychologically sound and mature will not be unduly disturbed by the presence or absence of a casket, open or closed, by viewing a burial or not, if they make their own choice. Most of us know our own coping powers and will invent proper strategies near death if allowed the freedom.

A wave toward cremation seems to be sweeping through larger sectors of our well-educated and more liberal population. Religious barriers are down and prices are attractive through newly invented methods and competitive markets. In addition to financial considerations, ecological concerns and the abhorrence of traditional burial rites seem responsible for the wave. Recently I noticed an ad in a college newspaper offering cremation for $25.00 "without pollution of air or land" under the banner "All men are cremated equal."

The visceral reaction of most Americans to cremation is rarely neutral. People seem either to believe in it and insist upon it for themselves, or they find it abhorrent. Many can mentally accept its worth who cannot allow its reality for themselves. For those nurtured on a steady experience of burial, cremation might seem to minimize tradition or the worth of the body as a temple of the human spirit. Often reluctance toward cremation is no more than a fear of losing mastery over the body by those unable to fathom that they will be gone when cremation occurs. I still find it quite impossible to conceive of my own death or burial without envisioning myself as present, watching my grave or cremating fires.

Funeral directors falter nervously in an open discussion of the cremation revolution. Theirs is a business geared to burial in the ground or in crypts and they understandably blanche at any promotion of simple cremation without embalming or casket, while pretending they only want whatever people want. It is not a moral or even an esthetic conflict, purely economic, as witnessed by how willingly undertakers co-operate with competitive crematoriums when casket and embalming precede a fiery disposition.

To survive and prosper, the funeral industry may have to regear its entire approach and resources. People will always need help near death, but not always embalming, cosmetics, caskets, graves and crypts or mausoleums. And if my interviews and observations are correct, the time for young funeral directors to begin a reform is yesterday. The young I question have few funeral or burial hang-ups that suggest they will be satisfied with former customs. Hang-ups may develop with age, but presently their sense of the sacred is not tied to bodies, caskets, cemeteries or giant mausoleums. Instant cremation with ashes strewn over the Atlantic or the Rockies makes more sense to most.

Benevolent dreamers among the young see massive, iron-fenced cemeteries in the heart of teeming neighborhoods as a criminal use of valuable territory man needs for better purposes. Acres of aged and rock-marked graves are seen as useless memorials to an ancient past the young choose not to revere. Their ecological sensitivities are offended and their moral outrage is ignited by the sight of land squandered on the dead. They cannot grasp why cemeteries could not double as parks or playgrounds by day and as backgrounds for musical concerts or drama festivals by night. In Vienna, Austria, some of the world's finest music can be heard in the city's burial grounds. The young are beginning to tell of seeing far more of the sacred in family laughter and joy, in inspirational art and music, in drama and in little children's playing feet than in the spookiness that haunts our traditional cemeteries. Gone is the fear of offending God by trespassing on graves or by laughing happily where yesterday tears and silence seemed reasonably proper. When offered the opportunity many young couples would see no contradiction in being married where mom and dad are buried and holding the reception nearby. Not like at Forest Lawn where chapels and euphemisms hide the realities of death, but on grass near tombstones where a new sense of reverence would not make death seem unduly stark or unreal.

The death blow to our barbaric funereal customs is how many youngsters view cremation. They fail to realize why huge crypts or mausoleums should house dead bodies when the living poor nearby have no proper homes. The young know little about the history of our burial practices, almost nothing of the resurrection from the dead and the second coming of Christ. And when they do, they differ with our conclusions. They admit man is a sacred being while disagreeing that the former physical receptacle of a man deserves or warrants such adoration and costly care. Maybe some believe the youth revolution is over. I see it as only gone quiet. Their assault on archaic death practices may never grow noisy, but I predict it will become increasingly insistent, economically.

Is it possible to insure the effectiveness and beauty of a family funeral? Sensitive and creative planning are a must if rites are not to slip into the traditional rut offered by some clergy to all who are indifferent. Before all else, a beautiful funeral should respect and reflect the desires and beliefs of the deceased. Funerals well may be for the living but they are the first opportunity the living have to show love and respect for the dead. How often I watched religious survivors use the funeral rites of an irreligious relative to proselytize their own beliefs. Priests would return from a funeral to tell how they "made those bastards think" at the obsequies for "an old reprobate" as nonconformers were called. Agnostics and atheists, no longer able to escape or disavow, provided ready platforms for zealous survivors to propagate their wares.

And the opposite is true as well. Disbelieving survivors will deny the believing dead any final right to religious rites that had mattered much. I sometimes saw offspring, who had drifted from their familial faith, obstruct religious burial for dedicated parents, apparently fearful of drawing too close.

Clergymen summoned to perform burial rites have an obligation to learn about the deceased and his family as deeply as time permits. Especially is this important when the clergyman is a stranger. The clergyman's aim ought to be to include the family life-style in the service, honoring their needs and wishes, avoiding what might easily upset, emphasizing what would inspire. Prayers aplenty for praying people, scriptures for the biblical, brevity for the impatient, wide latitude for individual differences, without doing violence to his personal beliefs. To contract to conduct a funeral means to instruct and console within the family's frame of values and not within the clergyman's own. Hopefully they can be almost the same.

When clergy have no sensitivity to family needs, no time to listen carefully and plan constructively, better not to engage them. Lack of planning can only result in cool, traditional ceremonies geared to every dead man in the past three hundred years, or to goofs and embarrassment. One undertaker tells of having heard so many identical eulogies that the first two people he plans to avoid in heaven are Sts. John and Paul. Almost daily he hears in canned eulogies all they had to say.

Most morticians know it well, but still fear admitting openly that the role of clergyman can easily be bypassed at most funerals. You do not need a license or ordination to bury, only to marry. When people were less skilled in public speaking and when the clergy had something distinctive to offer, the ministerial role was more vital. It still is when people want complicated liturgy included in the funeral rites. But the clergy can sometimes be only the easiest to obtain of several bad choices.

What do you do when you do not want a clergyman to conduct? Sometimes the funeral director himself makes a wise and willing substitute, knowing the family and experienced by years of observing the best and poorest in funeral rites. Or in almost any audience today there are friends or relatives capable of presiding effectively. All that is needed is a form or a structure, and the entire ceremony falls easily into place. Teachers and foremen, union leaders and salesmen, these are only a few of the dozens of occupations now practiced in addressing groups.

Several friends could touch on family memories. Prayerful people would gladly lead prayers and singers could provide favorite hymns or ballads, leading the group in chorus. The dramatic could read a poem or scripture. Maybe an uncle would choose to heal family wounds while skirting sore spots, adding the touch of reality professional eulogizers can only imitate. Many Jewish families and Hollywood stars have followed similar humanistic and unritualistic plans for years.

Most honest men are so weary of hearing lying eulogies that only tempt them to pry open the casket to insure they attended the right funeral. The glory of a man does not rest in how unrealistically good or great he sounds when dead, but rather in how well he managed to live with all his eccentricities and weaknesses. None of my friends could stand up under honest scrutiny if measured against an idealized Christ or any mythological saint. Eulogies struggle to make us admire those we only loved. They hold a woman up for adoration when the best we can do is to understand the love beneath her bitchiness. They measure men in heavenly terms when it was their kindly earthiness we treasured. When everyone who dies is sainted equally, as they usually are in modern eulogies, then there is no point in sanctity, no uniqueness, no use of striving for it or in telling of its merits, since all men will sound holily the same.

Clumsiness can be forecast where relatives and friends participate in funerals. Open tears will accompany words and bad taste will not be a stranger. A touch of humane earthiness will show, a tone so sorely lacking in the sterile rituals that have become routine at funerals. The unskilled will not know where to find quotes from John and Paul, or Psalm 23, or any ritual songs and prayers that serve only to keep us in touch with the past while generating huge sighs of relief when they are over.

Regretfully, I know how they will bury my parents and most of my religious friends. For Mom and Dad a monsignor will be summoned, maybe even a bishop, to enact rites sacred in their longevity and of little meaning to most in attendance. There will be liturgy in English now, talk of final resurrection, tribunals, days of wrath, salvation, beatific vision and eternal rest, words no more intelligible now than they were when chanted in Latin. The Knights of Columbus might parade in uniform, swords extended at appropriate times, and maybe soldiers will trumpet taps.

After all important institutions have had their way and say, I would so much like to be part of another service, a liturgy for all who cared and would understand. We would gather around the casket or near a picture, in the home the departed left. Everyone could have a say but nobody would be forced to fake it, each telling the impact of one human life upon the self. At Dad's funeral I hope one of his boys would dare sing the songs he used to wake us up for school, "Rise and Shine" or "Deep in the Heart of Texas," imitating Dad's incredible voice, tuneless, resounding louder and further than any voice I ever heard. Then we would pass pictures, Dad in boxing trunks, on his wedding day, skinny during the depression and the picture in the paper on Father's Day with seven sons.

At Mother's funeral I hope someone would tell about the night her giant carbuncle broke and seven little medics, ages four through seventeen, daubed her neck with cotton, while she laughed hysterically and scolded us all at once. Or maybe someone would tell of that proud night when all seven of us accompanied her to the frozen swamp where she donned her figure skates for the first time in twenty years and cut figure eights before fourteen begoggled eyes.

Maybe some might need a beer or a belt before they could talk freely or shed the tears that would grease their tongues. Too bad we are so far from freedom near death that we need help to talk of things that truly matter, dogs and vacations, sad times and good, family fights and eccentric neighbors. Our efforts would be to emphasize life here and how much it meant and means, instead of doing what rituals seem to do, deny the only life we ever knew together in favor of a future life we still cannot comprehend.

At first it will be hard to demythologize our funerals and substitute more human and meaningful ways to bury our dead. But one such funeral would cause the courage and daring to try many others. Now, our cultural traditions only approve of solemnity and glumness at the time of death. Seriousness predominates. Why must all funeral liturgy be so damned serious? After all, if we do not believe in God, life here is all we have to celebrate. If we do believe, man will soon resurrect into a new and richer life of eternal happiness. In either case there is much cause for celebration after the pain and shock of loss has partially cleared and we are regaining our perspective.

It is all right to smile near death, even to laugh. God is said to have made the anteater and the horned toad. Each time I gaze on them I smile, knowing somehow it's all right to be human enough to smile, even to laugh, around anything human or divine. Even around death. God made funny-looking animals and he made man weak enough to die.

# 11.
# Life Beyond?

Night was coming. Two American soldiers lay under a tree in an open jungle bunker, mortally wounded. The air was chilly.

"I wish the priest would find us," Malozzi muttered.

"I'm glad you're here," replied Brewer.

"I know I'm gonna die soon and I have so many sins ta confess."

"Yeah, I'm gonna flake out soon, too, and I need to talk to you."

Darkness came. Malozzi tried to make his priestless peace with God, whispering softly: "O my God, I'm heartily sorry for havin' offended Thee and I detest all my sins because I dread the loss of heaven and the pains of hell, but most of all because they offend Thee, my God, Who art all good and deservin' of all my love . . ."

"Hey, Maz, what are you saying?"

"I'm tellin' God I'm sorry, tryin' ta make an act of perfect contrition like we're supposed ta do when no priest comes for confession."

"What can I do?"

"Nothin', except maybe say a prayer for me."

"I can't. I don't pray. I never figured out if there is a God or not."

"Wow! At least ya could pray just in case there is. Are you some kinda atheist or somethin'?"

"Naw, I just don't know. I've heard so much rapping about religion I just can't understand the whole scene, but I'm sure glad you're here."

"I'm glad you're here, too, but I sure wish a padre would find us. I'd feel lots better confessin'."

Malozzi struggled to light a cigarette and passed it to Brewer. Pain wracked his body as he lit another one for himself. Brewer uncovered his canteen and both sipped a few drops. Malozzi kept whispering under his breath.

"What are you saying now?"

"That same prayer."

"Afraid your God didn't hear you?"

"Naw, afraid I didn't mean it as much as I could. I wanna be sure I'm sorry."

"Well, are you?"

"I think so, but I keep thinkin' I'd probably live the same way if I came over here again. It's hard ta say you're sorry for things ya liked."

"How can you be sorry for things you enjoyed and would do all over again if you had a chance?"

"I'm not sure but they were sins, those girls, the drugs, the suds I stole . . . and yer supposed ta be sorry."

"Aw, that's just being a man. Don't apologize for that.

You were a good man and still are, take it easy on yourself. I'm sure your God will understand."

"Naw, you don't unnerstand. All those things were mortal sins and Cathliks go ta hell for doin' them. They know better."

"I could never believe a God who'd send a guy like you to hell. I did the same things and I don't worry. I never hurt anybody and that's what matters. I paid the girls and took the drugs on the quiet. They helped a lot to keep me going and so did the brew I stole."

"Yeah, but I still wish the chaplain would get here. I'd feel better ta confess and have the last rites. It's so scary."

There was a long silence. Both were still bleeding badly. Then Brewer heard Malozzi mumbling softly, still talking to his God when suddenly the sounds stopped. He didn't dare look. He knew. He stared straight up, counting stars, trying not to think.

Now Brewer felt terribly alone and frightened. He had never been alone with a dead body. Fear and chill caused violent shivers. He knew he had only hours himself, maybe minutes. Home and Mom and Betsy flooded his thoughts. He wanted to say a little prayer for Malozzi. It would not cross his lips, dying in his mind.

Brewer wondered what might happen to him after death. He wondered where Malozzi was now. Was part of him living somewhere in the beyond or was all of him sleeping here forever? He was momentarily tempted to make peace with Malozzi's God until his mind raced past the fears. He now felt flashes of exhilaration all over like when facing a new experience, a blind ski slope, a new front to attack or skydiving for the first time. No guilt, only pain in his legs and lower torso where the mine had struck.

Brewer was walking down Main Street in his old neighborhood, waving, hand in hand with Betsy, still mildly puzzled over what lay beyond, when his breath stopped. There was a soft and quizzical smile on his face when buddies found them.

Is there any kind of life after death? Can we ever know for certain? Part of me believes with Malozzi while another part wonders and doubts with Brewer. Other parts inside me relate to the amusing contradictions among philosophers and theologians and equally to the nervousness found in humble worriers. Many times the question seems the most important in life and at other times too unimportant to ask. One thing is certain. No religion has yet succeeded in providing evidence sufficient to convince more than a fraction of mankind of its point of view, and only a somewhat larger fraction of its own followers.

I seem to have at least four heads working inside mine on the question of afterlife. I can never be quite positive of my own position, since it depends on which head is working at the moment.

My scientific head views man as only another animal, more advanced cerebrally, but as certain to die and decay as any lesser species. The cat lady in our block predicts a feline heaven for her forty pets and the pigeon lady in the downtown square claims to believe in a celestial aviary. But most men are convinced that animals simply die, and that is all. My scientific head pictures man reunited with the creatures and elements in the world he inhabited. "Remember man that thou art dust and unto dust thou shalt return."

This scientific head grew recently. For years my view of life was singlemindedly religious until this new head evolved gradually to provide inner reassurance around scientists who seem so secure in disbelieving afterlife, so smugly satisfied in death as an end to man. I cannot help but notice that most scientists I meet are wealthy enough to avoid the poverty and human degradation from which so much belief in heaven seems to flower. Few emotions accompany my scientific thinking, only a general uneasiness as science negates beliefs I held so long, and a sense of relief that I no longer need to bother with those moral codes that receive their punch from man's concern with afterlife. No hell.

On occasion my religious head still works. It can still plunge across the vacuum of convincing evidence, resolving contradictions, needily accepting the dreams and promises of prophets and evangelists. How simple life becomes. In their words of hope and instant purpose, all memories surge back from childhood, reminding me how those holy words stilled all childhood fears of death. When my religious head presides, I also feel mild twinges of fear for hell. As I read the sacred sources they were as forthright on hell as on the glories of heaven. Narrow the road to heaven, wide the path to hell and many who walk on it.

It could be comforting to withdraw into this head again, exclusively. The Jesus people do, and I sometimes envy their peaceful plunge into that "absurdity" they call faith. No doubts, not even any real questions, only firm and final guidelines. Yet, I hold back. For years I watched, even participating, as churches toyed with man's fear of punishment in afterlife, leading simple believers into paths of incredible moral rigidity and pettiness under a banner marked love.

If ever again I lop off all other heads to think religiously, I want belief to be free choice instead of fear or a habit begun before I could walk or talk. I want any faith I accept to flow from the nobler parts of self, and certainly not from a need to escape the tiring search for truth about an afterlife.

*213*

My third head is philosophical, sometimes even mystical. Plato, Aquinas, John of the Cross and Immanuel Kant are heroes here, as I quietly muse over their arguments for the immortality of the human soul. Sometimes it seems I can prove by abstract reasoning that man will live forever. His soul seems immaterial, spiritual and simple, indestructible. When I cease musing and reenter the world of flesh and machines, the arguments fade. All such arguments become unreal and unworkable in my total world where babies laugh, puppies frolic and people love.

So of late I conclude my philosophic meditations by reading one of my favorite philosophers, Soren Kierkegaard. "Honor to learning and honor to one who can treat the learned question of immortality in a learned way. But the question of immortality is *not* a learned question. It is a question of the inner existence, a question which the individual must confront by looking into his own soul." Right on, Soren! You make my fourth head seem sane.

This fourth head is not all head. It is partly heart. It works overtime when I read of slaughter in Vietnam or when I meet a man like Don. Don is only twenty-one now but will never walk or talk again. For five years he has been unable to do little more than lie in bed immobilized and stare. He can read in a mirror perched overhead while turning pages with a gimmick in his mouth, but cannot share his thoughts or even his reactions to mirrored television. He cannot even laugh and only barely smile. A modern hermit, involuntarily.

When visiting Don, I rap and rap, ostensibly to entertain, actually hoping to shield myself from the bitterness and futility in his eyes. All the while my fourth head is fashioning an afterlife, at least for Don. He deserves another chance at living, a chance to shed his withering body and to walk, talk and run, if only with saints and cherubs. Or maybe with a God who knows and permits his plight.

Along quiet streets I sometimes reflect on all the other "Dons" behind closed doors, the crippled and the slow, the aged and insane, all the unfortunates no human institution has yet learned to handle humanely and with happiness. I imagine, too, the prisoners of love or circumstance who tend their half-living charges, some in joy and peace, some in resentment, all with tedium and strain.

Love is mentioned so liberally today, yet the major tribute of supportive love we offer the "Dons" is "Hang on!" or "Keep up the fight!" maybe promising an afterlife where all tears will wash away. My fourth head could more easily accept a godless world without an afterlife, if staunch advocates of human love alone found better ways to help the Dons, the retarded and the old. Their human love would be more real than windy words if they showered it on those who cannot reciprocate with the same intensity they claim to shower it on those who can. I could better understand the rage of antiwar radicals if I saw them now nursing the paraplegics who took their place in the front lines.

Meanwhile, I listen respectfully to disclaimers of an afterlife while my fourth head secretly erects a place where Don will find all wrongs put right. His only "fault" was to dive into waters of unknown depth. My sense of justice and fair play necessitate a hereafter where Don will have another chance.

There are other voices, too, but none are convincing enough to make me believe I have more heads. After visiting a new place, a European castle or an Irish hamlet, I sometimes feel I was there before in a prior life. Often in meeting a total stranger, a feeling sweeps over me, we were friends before, another time, another place. Occasionally, engrossed in a movie or television, I feel strangely at home in medieval times, in a Swedish village or marching in the Civil War.

In a thanatology class of 156 students, seven claimed a firm belief in man's reincarnation into another form of life on earth, animal or human. I share experiences that lead to such a conclusion, maybe not as intensely, but I interpret the data differently. I see my feelings of similarity and identity with persons, places and former times as no more than deeply human bonds that link all sensitive men and women of every age and locale. Never have I needed to conclude that I existed some place on earth before or ever will again.

Of late I hear astrological voices speak of possibilities that the entire universe is man's eternal playground. I hear of union with higher forms of life, of attractive forms of reincarnation on other planets or of being whisked after death into planetary playgrounds for unimagined delights.

Now I am humble enough to listen respectfully, whereas before I could only join fellow believers in pigeon-holing all astrologers as kooks, while snickering at wise men through history who thought configurations of stars affected earthly life. At present, astrological voices are too many and too divergent for me to follow. When I listen to their cacophony I feel transported back to an ecumenical meeting of many years ago, only I can have more tolerance for astrologers than for theologians, since the universe is understandably more difficult to interpret univocally than a Bible or a Koran.

I do not obstruct any astrological voice, nor even parapsychological voices that talk of spiritualism and states of altered consciousness that bring immortality, yet the main lesson I learn is how modern man needs to grasp for new purpose and dignity as the world makes him feel increasingly nameless, faceless and useless. New and insightful meaning can be found in the signs of birth, new identity with important people and a new morality for making decisions without fear of hell. I guess my current preference is to look for meaning a bit closer to home in my own experience and in the folks I know.

The conclusions from my fourth head are, I know, little more than projections from my own mind and heart. Promise of a future life supplies meaning for the empty spots I find in human existence. Poverty in ghettos, boredom, war and disease, racism and despair, all will disappear in the eternity of my hopes. Behavioral scientists cite the self-fulfilling prophecy as being responsible for so much of what happens in life. I do not think it mad to hope that my concerns and aspirations for humankind might well cause justice and peace in my life hereafter.

I would feel silly, maybe even slightly stupid, if I were alone in the playful enjoyment of this childlike game to create your favorite eternity. It is the identical game little people play in youthful fantasy and the child in each of us continues to play throughout life. Little boys build castles in their fantasies while daddies lose themselves in a televised game or show, plunging for a final touchdown, dunking a layup in overtime or rescuing a damsel lost among thieves. Moms remake dads and marriages in ecstatic reveries before television soap operas while little girls record in journals romantic dreams of love with dozens of different suitors. Recollections of the past and all plans for the future only serve to add to our present what we most seem to need: love, kindness, punishment, excitement or adventure. Ask about my childhood or my golden years, and I will regale you with stories that tell much about my present needs.

Religious leaders have played this same exciting game for centuries and are still deeply engrossed. Under the mantel of deep scholarship and with special guidance from on high, the leaders of world religions read their prophets and divines with astoundingly different conclusions.

Most Western preachers or theologians read in their sacred sources of an afterlife for all, heaven for the blessed, hell for the accursed. Others find in the same texts that afterlife is reserved for believers, or find little evidence of afterlife at all, or only evidence of a heaven. Learned and holy interpretations include countless other important variables like purgatory and limbo, the duration of hell and the reality of a particular judgment instantly after death, not to mention the almost infinite variety of paths by which eternal locations are reached. Catholics might reach hell by using contraceptives while other sects might be damned if they don't.

Religious sages might be more learned than most others, debating Hebrew or Greek meanings, quoting commentaries and Dead Sea Scrolls, but to me, who used to be one of them, they are like the rest of us, tiny tots engrossed in our wonderful game. No question here of any man's sincerity. I only believe religious teachers are as right or wrong as the rest of us who might find acceptable meaning in eternal sleep, in reincarnation or in interplanetary playgrounds. Their only advantage is that whole nations and races, whole cultures and civilizations, fashioned their religious beliefs into unifying creeds for the humble to publicly follow. They also had monarchs and armies to enforce their fantasies with jails and swords. The swords could lop off disbelieving or nonconforming heads, but they could not prevent other heads from playing this game in private.

In short, we might easily conclude that nobody knows for certain about an afterlife. Instead, I choose to hold with Kierkegaard that every man knows for himself within his inner soul. Maybe nobody can ever know what to believe for anyone besides himself. Near death, true belief in what you sincerely hold will bring peace and any promise you need for your future. Scientists, philosophers and theologians are forever arguing each other into contradictions, and the man who claims to know what is correct for others to believe must leap across the centuries of conflicting and contradicting views.

This conclusion makes far more sense to me than all the deathbed conversions where men tried to die in a faith unknown until the last, or in one they cared not or dared not to live by, a final greedy grasp, willing to pretend in order to steal a possible heaven. Just in case.

A major reason why Americans find it so easy to blithely dismiss all hint of an afterlife is that continued contentment seems possible in the present. Pain and poverty are far away from most and seem conquerable, while advances in medicine make death seem more distant. Life within an affluent society, or at least near one, dissipates so much of the human need to dream of heaven. The promise of plenty in this life, even if only made in movies and ads, blots out much thought of dying, perfuming all death, distracting from afterlife with rich fantasies for now and tomorrow. Man madly concentrates on making heaven on earth, believing it possible, if only, if only . . .

Of late, the voices in my several heads are increasingly still. I am increasingly satisfied to only feel my present feelings, my fears, my pangs for more, my hopes, my panic, allowing them to rummage around inside, without running to my fantasies for a cure or an explanation. Then I begin to wonder if the whole question of an afterlife makes any difference at all. I find that I am no more or less moral by believing in it than I am by being indifferent, no happier, no kinder, no more peaceful. Maybe there is no life after death, only restful and dreamless sleep, and all we have is what we feel within us and what we see around us. Maybe there is nothing more than our bodies and minds, our friends, our work and hobbies, our growing older daily, our pains and wars, our human joys and death. And as I learn to love life and self and those nearby, finding new appreciation by study and reflection on death, maybe these are enough.

I am prepared to think momentarily with you that life

here on earth is all we have. I can admit my own hopes for an afterlife are dreams that will never come true. Can you shed for the moment any myths about afterlife that might be lingering in your head? How would your life be changed? I think not much at all. The unhappily married think they might run to a divorce court. Teetotalers think they might tilt a few too many and the lusty envision risky affairs. The angry think they might murder someone in vengeance. On the contrary, I find by experience that men remain morally the same without belief in afterlife, and maybe nonbelievers work harder to make this world a moral and happier place because it is all they have.

Belief in any kind of an afterlife seems impossibly unreal even to those who claim unwavering faith. I used to enjoy asking groups of staunch believers a series of questions. "How many believe in heaven?" All hands raised high. "How many believe heaven is eternal and perfect happiness?" Most hands this time. "How many are perfectly happy on earth?" Almost no hands. "How many want to leave for heaven today?" Never more than a few hands, usually wrinkled ones.

Would no afterlife alter the fears most men have of dying? I am convinced it would not change deathbed fears more than a tiny bit, probably reducing dying fears if anything, since dying believers reflect more anxiety over loss of life and possible punishment than a sense of joy at joining their God in heaven.

An afterlife where man lives pleasurably without his body is beyond my comprehension. I can admit its possibility but I cannot long for it or even know if I would want it. In sermons and lectures I used to describe life without a body, using Cardinal Newman's poem "The Dream of Gerontius" wherein he undertakes the formidable task of describing the moments after the soul leaves the body and ascends before Christ in particular judgment. With all of his considerable literary and philosophical skills, Newman failed. And I with him. Either we use figures of descriptive speech which demand a body or our explanations lose everyone except the deeply metaphysical.

Poets and evangelists all face the same problem. So do novelists and preachers. Either they resort to an abstract imagery devoid of emotional and physical dimensions or they use that childlike imagery of fantasy which demands the presence of a body which lies molding in a grave or in the sea. Their heaven of abstraction has no attraction nor could any heaven delight a man without a body, as far as I can fathom. I think of the billions who have already died in the thousands of years man has inhabited this earth. Then I find little sense in turning on to tales of sylvan glens, mansions, verdant meadows, harp music, banquets or angelic choirs, not even to the humorous quips of black folk preachers who see heaven as "a never ending line of fried chicken, black-eyed peas and corn pone—without a white man in sight."

After careful analysis and reflection, I am convinced that belief in an afterlife brings no special peace to the dying that cannot be found by firm adherence to any other belief. We meet religious people well enough disposed to die in dignity and in peace, yet we also meet nonreligious people with equal dispositions near death. It is not the content of a man's creed that makes him confident and peaceful near life's brink. It is more the quality of his act of believing that counts.

Faith or belief are not the sole privileges of religious people as I once thought. Faith is simply that total commitment of the entire person to an ideal, a way of life, a set of values, to anything or anyone beyond the narrow limitations of myself: God, mankind, the poor, science, human relations, growth and development, anything capable of bringing meaning and purpose to life.

Too readily we classify as believers only those who wish

they were or claim to be, anybody who says "I believe." Belief can be surface or shallow, a childhood dream or a parental wish, a family tradition or what society demands. Or it can be deeply imbedded in every portion of one's personality and being. Belief can be thoughtless following, love for a preacher or a balm to our fears as easily as being what I considerately choose after prayer and reflection. True believers are those who internalize and live what they claim to believe. The truths they securely hold are wound tightly into the total self, altering every deed, coloring every view, influencing every relationship. Onlookers will know almost infallibly once they are in the presence of a true believer. He is not loud or defensive and has no need to argue pettily or to compel imitation. His firm belief in someone or something transcendent only invites admiration and imitation. This quality of believing is any man's major asset in facing his own death.

Unfortunately, it is intensely difficult today for belief to go deeper than the lips. Commitment has become the rascal of our times, easily evading all but the truest of true believers. Believers in science will often leave their creed at the laboratory door and believers in God leave theirs in church. Those who claim to uphold the dignity of man will often hold up any man they can, while believers in eternal sleep sometimes live as if their life were to be measured by an avenging God. Many of us have differing sets of beliefs for any occasion. True belief that will bring solace near death is measured more in actions during life than by loud protestations.

Belief in any higher meaning or worth in life can lend a special beauty to a man's life, even when we violently disagree with the truth value of his creed. I can admire the glow on the face of the nun and the vibrations of sincerity from the Jehovah's Witness who pushes her frightened little boy to preach at my front door. I feel deep respect for the dynamism in the man for whom science is a mystical or religious experience and the serenity of one who finds his major meaning in learning to relate and better communicate with other men. The true believer, after I sort out my personal feelings toward the tenets in his creed, reflects to me a sense of inner worth, a spirit of mission and purpose, a confident conviction and a tranquil assurance. Near death the true believer knows why he lived and can face the unfinished tasks of his life with his vision in clear focus. Because true belief brought perspective into life, so will it endow death with a more satisfying point of view. And no matter how wonderful religion may be for many, it is only one of the many ways to gain this stature of true belief.

When death draws near, the dying frequently begin to wonder about the wisdom of a return to a childhood belief or a former faith, even about the quick adoption of a faith from someone they admire. Dying people confess to doubting whether they could make such a transition or if they might soon feel compelled to make a deathbed switch by the weight of fear and guilt. Their conflict is compounded by a human noble streak that makes many men reluctant, near death, to clutch desperately for truths they abandoned or denied in the heat of life. The dying will often appear bullheaded in their refusal to change beliefs when they are only attempting to be honest in not becoming a parasite for peace. There is nothing so wrong in a last minute switch to please a religious wife or husband, or maybe a mother, but I have great doubts about the faith and the love of a person who would occasion such a change for even the noblest of reasons.

Any belief fashioned in life is a good belief for facing

death, provided it fits well enough to be one's own. Borrowing beliefs can be as risky as borrowing money. Any creed that has become a part of a person's life-style, that was sincerely held and lived by, that took the believer beyond the solipsism of self, can serve the dual purpose any belief seems to serve near death. First, it will grant purpose and meaning through the agony and pain, through the hopelessness and fear. Nothing ever seems quite so difficult if there is some reasonable purpose behind it. And any transcendent belief confers reason on life and its passing. Secondly, belief will prepare the dying to meet any God with whom they might be spending an eternity. Try as I might, I cannot conceive of any all-knowing, all-caring God of whatever denomination who would admire a cheap and fearful switch near death more than a firm adherence to beliefs gained in the struggle of life.

Especially near death, the problem with making a commitment resurrects. No matter the beauty of the ideals or values we lived by, we always seem eager to wonder if something better will come, if a more rewarding creed is not around the corner. This deathbed version of the puritan ethic has become an American bug. In life, it nibbles away at enduring commitment, at marital vows, at job stability and at loyalty in friendship or fealty to country. And at death, it gnaws at the validity of our own beliefs.

Skeptics and agnostics can find peace at the end, plus assurance of safety in any possible hereafter, if their search is their creed and they are sincerely committed to it. When any quest for truth is real, not mere talk or laziness, not indifference or being too busy, it can reward the searcher with all the wealth found in true belief. We can help if we give him confidence in the validity of his own choice. One of the noblest styles of life conceivable is that of sincere searching for truth. No God I ever read about or could love would disown a creature who lived in honest quest for a purpose he could totally endorse. Nor would any God reject a creature who found out too late his searching was dishonest or his heart disinterested or distracted. When life is ebbing away, knowing that you tried is faith enough to still the very human fears at dying and to satisfy any God who allowed his people to become so confused and his world so confusing.

Is there an afterlife for Malozzi, for Brewer, for you or for me? Being a true believer as best I can makes the whole question less vital for me. Undue preoccupation with the "whether" of an afterlife has ruined untold numbers of lives with unnecessary fears. It has split families and impoverished tribes which put riches and even people into tombs. It has put too much magical power into the hands of religious leaders, often distracting them from godliness. It has deferred the social progress of mankind in dealing with poverty, ignorance, disease and war, deferring until another life the insistent needs and demands of today. About the only good I can see is that our overpreoccupation has been good for the economy.

As I finish writing, I feel like I am burying a good friend. I feel afraid to shovel the last bit of dirt on his grave for fear it is all over, there is no more. I am fearful of writing the final words because then you will know how little I know about the mystery of death.

I think I will go back and visit Don. I want to make another effort to offer him something more than cheery promises for a possible future happiness. I am certain that together we can find much more meaning and purpose for this present. Maybe seeing and breathing are all the joys Don will ever know, maybe not. But I for one am tired of telling the hapless and the poor about celestial peace and justice, neatly excusing myself from all the efforts required by the problems I see today on earth. I am weary of watching myself and others play no more than our wonderful game of fantasy, create your own afterlife.

Helping Don, who seems to have died quite some time ago, will help me face life as it is. I am ashamed how little I know about death and dying, but never have I enjoyed life more, dreamed more beautiful dreams each night, than when I began having courage to begin facing death.